BIDDULPH GRANGE

THE NATIONAL TRUST

BIDDULPH GRANGE

STAFFORDSHIRE

A VICTORIAN GARDEN REDISCOVERED

Peter Hayden

THE NATIONAL TRUST · GEORGE PHILIP

For Conrad Reginald Cooke, OBE,
great-grandson of Edward Cooke
and great-great-great-grandson of Conrad Loddiges

Published by George Philip Limited,
59 Grosvenor Street, London W1X 9DA,
in association with
The National Trust, 36 Queen Anne's Gate, London SW1H 9AS.

© Peter Hayden 1989

British Library Cataloguing in Publication Data
Hayden, Peter, *1928* –
    Biddulph Grange, Stafford: Victorian garden rediscovered.
1. Staffordshire. Biddulph – Visitors' guides
I. Title   II. National Trust
914.24'61

ISBN 0-540-01192-4

Printed in Hong Kong

FRONTISPIECE
View across the lake at Biddulph in spring, showing one
of the surviving wings of James Bateman's house.

Contents

Acknowledgements

I am indebted to many people for help in researching this book, particularly Reggie Cooke for generously making available to me the diaries of Edward Cooke and Jane Loddiges as well as other valuable material; Julian Gibbs and John Sales of the National Trust and Mavis Batey, Ray Desmond, Dr Brent Elliott and Dr Keith Goodway, all of the Garden History Society, for help on many occasions; Anthony Blacklay and Associates, architects, for the conjectural plan of the house in 1862; Philip Taylor of Anthony Blacklay and Associates for the front elevation of the Chinese temple; Jeremy Milln, the National Trust's archaeologist at Biddulph; Derek Wheelhouse for sharing his considerable knowledge of the history of Biddulph; Jack Charlton, the successor of Bateman's Congleton solicitor, for the loan of documents relating to the Biddulph and Knypersley estates; James Edleston of Bower, Edleston & Partners, architects, of Nantwich, Cheshire, for material relating to the rebuilding of the house by Thomas Bower in 1896; Mr and Mrs James Fletcher for the loan of the Heath family photograph albums; Fred Pointon for the loan of the diary of his great-grandfather, Luke Pointon, who was Robert Heath's head gardener at Biddulph Grange; Mrs Joyce Machin, the granddaughter of Luke Pointon, for the photograph of him organising the moving of a tree; the late Miles Hadfield, who was the first in recent times to draw attention to the importance of the garden; Robert Copeland and Mr F. W. H. Coles for the photograph of the Spode plate; Martyn Gregory for the photograph of Edward Cooke's painting of Glen Andred; John Munday, the leading authority on Edward Cooke, to whose book I look forward; Charles Foster, the Arley Hall Archivist and the Hon. Mrs Jane Foster, the Biddulph Grange Archivist; Andzrej Kostołowski for the text of Adam Moszynski's essay; and Esmond Ball, James Barfoot, David Bett, Krysia Bilikowski, David Brown, the Revd Robert Carter, the late Anne Ferris, Rodney Hampson, Dr John H. Harvey, Margaret Hemmings, Ian Moxon, Michael Pearman, Mr Perkins of Glen Andred, Brian Rittershausen, Dr T. V. Shulkina, Margaret Smith, Alan Taylor, Dr Hugh Torrens and Basil Williams.

I am also indebted for their help to the librarians, archivists and staff of the Chatsworth Settlement Trust, the Cheshire County Record Office, the

Herbarium Library at Kew, the Lindley Library, the Linnean Society, the London Borough of Hackney Archives Department, the Society of Antiquaries, the Staffordshire County Record Office and the William Salt Library in Stafford. I am most grateful for permission to reproduce material from their collections to the British Library, the Chatsworth Settlement Trust, Cheshire County Council, the Hon. Michael Flower of Arley Hall, the Linnean Society, the London Borough of Hackney Council, the National Maritime Museum, the Royal Botanic Gardens, Kew, the Royal Horticultural Society, the Royal Society, Staffordshire County Council, the Victoria and Albert Museum and the William Salt Library.

I owe a great deal to my editor, Lydia Greeves, for her patience and guidance, and to my wife for reading my typescript at various stages and for many valuable suggestions.

Finally I should like to acknowledge the contributions of all those who helped to save Biddulph Grange – the steering committee who kept hope alive by campaigning for its conservation; the officers and panel members of the National Trust concerned in its acquisition; and the National Heritage Memorial Fund, English Heritage and all those bodies and individuals whose donations have made possible the restoration carried out so far. I hope that many more will respond to the Trust's appeal, for considerable sums are still needed to complete the restoration and to ensure the future maintenance of the garden.

Peter Hayden

Grotesque animals by Edward Cooke, who designed many features in the garden at Biddulph Grange.

Introduction:
A Remarkable Survival

When I first visited Biddulph Grange twenty-five years ago I had no idea that so much of this remarkable garden had survived. I had seen old photographs of an extraordinary Egyptian pyramid of clipped yew, of a Chinese garden with a temple and a bridge of intricate design, and of a long dahlia walk backed by a yew hedge and divided by buttresses of yew, but I had imagined that all this must have disappeared during the many years since Biddulph Grange had become a hospital.

As I stood on the terrace on the south front that afternoon and looked across well-kept lawns to the lake and the many mature trees and shrubs beyond, it was clear that a great deal of James Bateman's famous garden was still there. True, the tall yew hedge and the dahlia walk had gone, but when I looked up the slope to the east I could see the Egyptian pyramid looking very much as it did in the photograph. It was one of the most striking examples of topiary work I had ever seen. Closer inspection was to show that the yew had been ingeniously planted at different levels to achieve its unique form.

Obelisks of yew and two pairs of handsome stone sphinxes guarded the stone-framed entrance to the pyramid. The tunnel beyond was long and gloomy and led to a small panelled chamber. Here, in a recess facing the entrance, one of the garden's many surprises lay in wait for me – a large stone monster squatting on its haunches, bathed in ruby light from coloured glass in the roof above. A few steps further on I emerged into the daylight to find that this was not the rear entrance of an Egyptian pyramid but the front door of a half-timbered cottage bearing the date 1856 and the letters JB and MB – the initials of James and Maria Bateman.

There was a complete change of scenery on the other side of the pyramid, for this was the pinetum, announced by two large stone pine cones flanking the path. But it was a pinetum with a difference, not merely a collection of trees but a very skilful piece of landscaping, with a walk winding between gently rising slopes on either side, excluding views of the areas beyond and forming mounds of different heights to set off the trees planted on them to advantage. The many fine trees which remained included a number of very large monkey puzzles, some Atlas cedars, Lebanon cedars, cypresses (chamaecyparis), pines, yews and

A plan of the garden at Biddulph Grange which accompanied a series of articles by Edward Kemp, the landscape gardener, in the Gardeners' Chronicle *in 1862.*

8

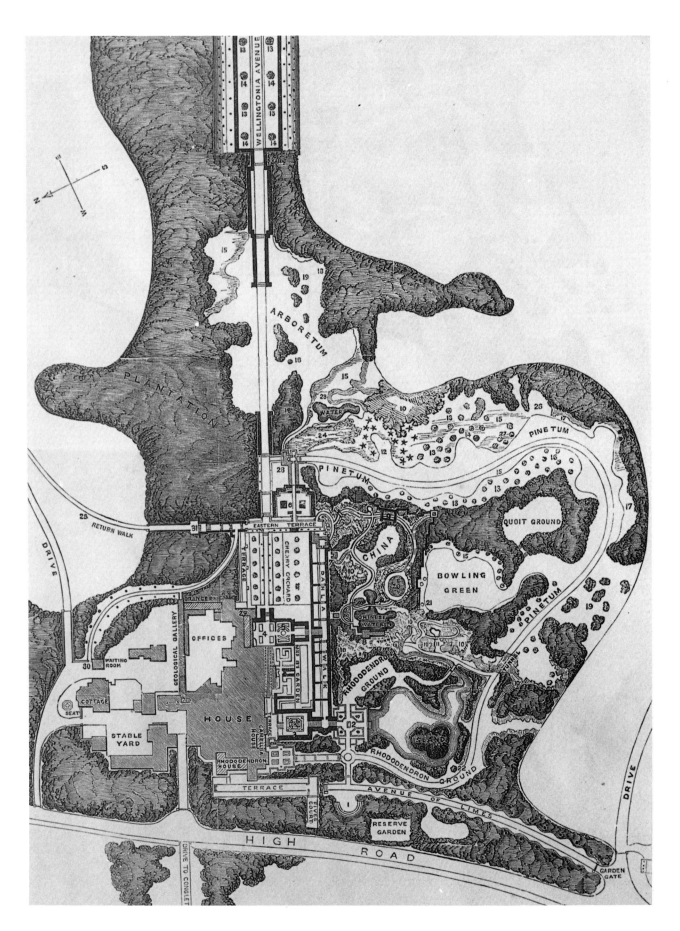

N
W E
S

WELLINGTONIA AVENUE

13 13
14 14
13 13
14 14

15
19 18

ARBORETUM

18

PLANTATION

16

15

WATER
23
10
24
12 13 13
13 15
26
27 PINETUM 17
15
13
16
13
15 17

25 RETURN WALK

DRIVE

31

23

6

EASTERN TERRACE

CHERRY ORCHARD

DAHLIA WALK

TERRACE

ORANGERY

29

GEOLOGICAL GALLERY

OFFICES

4

CHINA

10

10

10

CHINESE WATERS

8 TUNNEL

10 11 10

QUOIT GROUND

BOWLING GREEN

15

20

21

PINETUM

19

TUNNEL

30 WAITING ROOM

COTTAGE

SEAT

STABLE YARD

HOUSE

CAMELLIA HOUSE

TERRACE

RHODODENDRON HOUSE

MAZE OR BY GARDEN

TERRACE

FIVES COURT

5

2

RHODODENDRON GROUND

ISLAND

22

RHODODENDRON GROUND

1

AVENUE OF LIMES

RESERVE GARDEN

HIGH ROAD

DRIVE TO CONGLE

DRIVE

GARDEN GATE

9

hemlocks. There were also a few oaks, one of them a variegated species I had not seen before.

Had I turned off to the right through the trees I would have found the long-overgrown sites of the quoits ground and bowling green, but I followed the path and eventually reached the mouth of a tunnel in a mass of rock which led to the rhododendron ground. Here there were many large old rhododendrons and other shrubs, some impressive rocks and a view across the lake to the house. I could see that the main path led round the lake to the terrace, but I turned off through an opening in the rocks and found myself in a narrow glen, where a path followed a small stream beneath a towering rock-face. Bamboos, ferns, rhododendrons and other evergreens thrived in this sheltered and shady place.

At the end of the glen another tunnel through rock led to the greatest of the afternoon's surprises. From the complete darkness of a winding passage I was suddenly transported into China and standing on the terrace of the temple I had seen in the old photograph, with a view across an ornamental pool to a willow-pattern bridge set among bamboos, maples and a great variety of other plants. Exploring further I came across a giant stone frog, a porcelain lion, oriental archways, a pair of dragons fashioned in red ash in a semi-circle of grass and a sculpted ox towering over them and gazing across the pool. The path led on through a sheltered hollow surrounded by walls of tufa designed to protect moutan peonies, and then upwards through rock and fern to a brightly coloured pavilion – the joss house – and a long stone wall representing the Great Wall of China. From the parapet of a stone watch-tower I had a commanding view of the whole of the Chinese garden and was better able to appreciate how skilfully it had been secluded from the surrounding areas by high, densely-planted earth banks and rock-work. I had seen many Chinese garden buildings before, but this was the first time I had seen an entire Chinese garden. Other impressive features I saw that afternoon were a fine lime avenue leading to Biddulph church and an avenue of deodar cedars, terminated by an enormous stone vase, climbing the slope towards Biddulph Moor.

As I became better acquainted with the garden I was able to appreciate that all this varied and picturesque scenery was devised not just for its own sake, but in order to provide a great diversity of conditions in which to grow the widest possible range of plants, for James Bateman was one of the most enthusiastic and accomplished of plantsmen. When he was still in his twenties, before he started to make the garden at Biddulph, he was already recognised as an international authority on orchids, which he continued to cultivate in the hothouses of Knypersley Hall, the home of his parents, a mile or two away. His wife, Maria, shared his enthusiasm for gardening and together with Edward Cooke, the gifted painter and occasional landscape designer, they created one of our greatest gardens.

Their achievement is all the more remarkable in view of the garden's unpromising location at a height of between 500 and 600 feet, below the

One of the oriental gateways in the Chinese garden at Biddulph. Bateman appreciated the role of sunlight in the garden, particularly when seen through the leaves of his Japanese maples: 'They shine with a brilliant metallic reddish copper transparency that cannot be described.'

western edge of Biddulph Moor. The situation is exposed and the North Staffordshire climate rather cold and wet – 'hyperborean' was the word Bateman used to describe it in a letter to Sir William Hooker, the Director of the Royal Botanic Gardens at Kew – but he endeavoured to overcome this by providing each plant with the necessary degree of protection. 'By a happy arrangement of the surface of the ground', wrote Edward Kemp, the landscape gardener, in the *Gardeners' Chronicle* in 1856, 'and its formation into an infinite variety of hills and dales, nooks and recesses, a considerable amount of shelter and exposure, sunniness and shade, dryness and moisture, has been obtained in the most ingenious manner; and the plants selected and the positions adopted for them with a patient study of their wants and a careful regard for their healthy development, which takes the visitor completely by surprise.'

The Batemans were born in an age of botanical fervour. Towards the end of the eighteenth century and during the first decades of the nineteenth there was a great surge of interest in plants, and owners of gardens became increasingly intent on collecting and cultivating as many kinds as they could afford. At the same time the exploration of China, the Pacific, South Africa and the Americas resulted in many new plants being discovered, many of which were splendidly illustrated in botanical periodicals and were made available through the growing number of nurseries.

The making of a garden like Biddulph Grange depended not only on the skill of those who designed and planted it, but also on the collectors who went into unknown and often dangerous regions to find new plants; on the invention of a greatly improved method of transporting them; on the nurserymen who propagated them in far greater variety than any of our nurseries and garden centres today; and on arbiters of taste who led the way in the gardens they designed and in their writings. All these factors helped to provide the conditions in which Biddulph Grange could flourish.

The Chinese bridge and temple in 1905, when Biddulph Grange garden was still maintained to a very high standard by the Heaths.

ONE

A Passion for Plants

The garden historian Miles Hadfield considered Biddulph Grange an 'un-Victorian Victorian garden'. It is certainly not a typical Victorian garden, yet it is very much a garden of its time. Had James Bateman been born a century earlier, with sufficient means, he might well have invited 'Capability' Brown to North Staffordshire to improve not just the Biddulph Grange estate but the whole of the family's Knypersley estate as well. Brown would have sought to emphasise the best features of the place, arranging trees in plantations, clumps and as single specimens, introducing a serpentine river, a lake and, perhaps, a cascade, and bringing the grass of the landscape up to the walls of the house. A few exotic trees and shrubs would have appeared in the scheme, but for the most part he would have planted native species.

At the turn of the century the chosen landscaper might have been Humphry Repton. His treatment of the wider landscape would have been similar to Brown's – idealised Nature – but near the house, in line with his view of 'the mistaken taste for placing a large house in a naked grass field', there would have been a terrace and, in all probability, a garden of American plants, a rose garden and flower gardens. These additions would have reflected the generally quickening interest in the wealth of often spectacular new herbaceous plants, shrubs and trees which were by then reaching England from many parts of the world.

After Repton's departure from the scene, the most prominent figure in British gardening in the first half of the nineteenth century was John Claudius Loudon (1783–1843). Born and educated in Scotland, he moved to London at the age of twenty and, thanks to good connections as well as ability, soon established a successful practice as a landscape gardener; but the great influence he commanded rested mainly on the impressive range of his publications which appeared over a period of four decades. He travelled extensively in Great Britain and his journeys in Europe took him as far afield as Moscow, visiting gardens and studying the state of horticulture wherever he went. His *An Encyclopaedia of Gardening*, first published in 1822, remains the most comprehensive single-volume work of its kind; his magnificent eight-volume study of trees and shrubs, *Arboretum et Fruticetum Britannicum*, has still not been superseded; while his *Gardener's Magazine,* to which James Bateman contributed, was widely read by both amateur and professional gardeners.

While Brown and Repton had been engaged almost exclusively by the owners of considerable estates, Loudon was addressing a much wider audience, including many who had earned their new wealth and status during the Industrial Revolution and who were anxious to create fashionable gardens around their suburban villas. Most of the nation's gardening activity was now directed not at extensive landscaping but at making gardens of a more modest size in which to grow ornamental plants. The imitation of nature was no longer the guiding principle; rather, gardens should be seen as works of art. In the eighteenth century standards of taste had been considered to be absolute, with a widely shared commitment to a common ideal, but now taste was seen to be a matter of personal opinion, and this freedom to differ was at the root of the great diversity of nineteenth-century gardens.

Loudon, in *The Suburban Gardener,* wrote of the 'picturesque', the 'gardenesque' and the 'geometric' approaches to garden design. Picturesque imitation of nature was, he argued, acceptable provided that foreign trees, shrubs and plants were used, for they would show that the result was a work of art. The gardenesque style, on the other hand, concentrated on the display of individual plants rather than the overall effect. 'Trees, shrubs and plants in the gardenesque style are planted and managed in such a way as that each may arrive at perfection and display its beauties to great advantage as if it were cultivated for that purpose alone.' Each plant had to be given enough space to achieve its full potential without being crowded by its neighbours. Trees were often planted on mounds. Other components of the style were 'the smoothness and greenness of lawns; and the smooth surfaces, curved directions, dryness and firmness of the walks'. (After 1831 the smooth finish of the lawns could be maintained by Mr Budding's invention, the lawn mower.) The geometric style was a return to the formality which was universal before the introduction of landscape gardening. As the century progressed, brightly coloured dwarf bedding plants set out in elaborate patterns featured prominently in many gardens.

Plants were not, of course, the sole ornaments of gardens. There were fountains (which the eighteenth century had regarded as unnatural), statues, bowers and arches of trellis-work, sundials, rustic summer-houses and rustic furniture, while rock-work and root-work (using tree stumps in much the same way as rocks) were introduced in the wilder parts of the garden further from the house. But plants were the most important element, whether in shrubberies, flower-beds, flower-baskets and vases, or in conservatories. Such were the characteristic features of English gardens when James and Maria Bateman began work at Biddulph.

Loudon's own garden in London marks the difference between his approach to his *métier* and that of Brown and Repton. It was attached to a new semi-

15

detached villa, at 3 Porchester Terrace, Bayswater, and work began on the garden in 1823. Eventually 2000 species of plants, not to mention varieties, were grown on rather less than a quarter of an acre. The front garden and that of its neighbour were similarly planted, as Loudon described in *The Suburban Gardener*, 'to make both gardens, as well as both houses, appear as one, with a cedar of Lebanon, a walnut, a purple beech, a sweet chestnut and a wide range of flowering shrubs and trees to give a succession of flowers in spring and berries in autumn'. 'Almost all the kinds of trees and shrubs that could, in 1823 and 1824, be procured in the London nurseries' were represented in the garden, though roses were restricted to '100 select shrubs, chiefly standards and budded dwarfs'. Behind the railings of the front fence there was a row of variegated hollies, each plant a different variety. There was a veranda on two sides of the house, and against this were planted various magnolias, honeysuckles, roses, periwinkles, wistarias and other shrubs. On the veranda, sheltered by its glass roof, were figs, vines and roses, while between its pillars, in narrow boxes, stood small pots of flowers in bloom which were changed throughout the year.

Behind the house one bed was used for herbaceous plants, which were chosen to give the widest range of colours for as much of the year as possible. Other beds were devoted to florists' flowers, with many kinds of tulips, ranunculuses, anemones, pinks, carnations, primroses, polyanthuses and dahlias. There were more than 'fifty kinds of apples, nearly as many kinds of pears, and a corresponding number of plums and cherries, with some peaches, nectarines, apricots, figs and vines'. In the hothouses there was an equally impressive range of plants, many of them supplied by the Royal Botanic Gardens at Kew and by Loddiges' nursery at Hackney, in north-east London.

This garden was not, of course, intended as a pleasure ground, but was an experimental station where Loudon could study a very wide range of plants. They could not be given the space to allow them to reach perfection in the gardenesque manner, but, with so many plants available and new species arriving all the time, it was important for the leading horticultural writer of the day to get to know them.

J. C. Loudon's wife, Jane, was no less remarkable than her husband. He met her after reading her novel, *The Mummy*, an extraordinary piece of science fiction set in the twenty-first century with predictions of a steam-plough, a milking machine, air transport by balloon, communications by rocket, the political separation of England and Ireland and 'a patent steam coffee-machine, by which coffee was roasted, ground, made, and poured out with *ad libitum* of boiling milk and sugar, all in the space of five minutes'. Astonished to find that the mind behind such ideas was a woman's, he married her. She gave him invaluable assistance with his work as well as writing some notable gardening books on her own account, including *Gardening for Ladies*, *The Ladies' Companion to the Flower Garden* and *The Ladies' Flower Garden*, and founding and editing *The Ladies' Magazine of Gardening*.

Camellia maliflora, introduced from China in 1818, was probably grown in the camellia house at Biddulph.

17

Jane Loudon led the way for women to play an increasingly important role in the garden. In the seventeenth century the flower garden was often considered to be the province of women, but planning the landscaping of estates in the eighteenth century was seen as a man's occupation. The potter, Josiah Wedgwood, in a letter to his partner Thomas Bentley, reported a conversation he had had with 'Capability' Brown: 'I told him that my life was devoted to the service of the Ladys as his was to that of the Noblemen and Gentlemen.' But when flowers again became important in the garden, women reasserted themselves. Prince Pückler-Muskau, the German landscape gardener, wrote after visiting the Earl of Pembroke's garden at Wilton in 1828: 'The garden is extremely pretty and elegant: it reflects honour on English women of rank, that most of them are distinguished for their skill and taste in this beautiful art.'

Another much-admired garden laid out by a woman was that created by Mrs Louisa Lawrence on a two-acre site at Drayton Green, seven miles west of London. In *The Suburban Gardener*, Loudon presented it as a model to be followed, finding it 'remarkable for the very great variety it contains in a very limited space'. He praised the way she had introduced many small trees and rare and beautiful shrubs, combining them with flowers and climbers, or with rock-work, fountains, basketwork and other garden features. Mrs Lawrence also had one of the best collections of hothouse plants in London. Her catalogue of the plants in the garden listed 600 species and varieties of hardy herbaceous plants, 212 of hardy and half-hardy ornamental trees and shrubs, 200 varieties of heartsease, 500 of roses and 140 species and varieties of florists' pelargoniums. She was a leading exhibitor at the shows of the Horticultural Society and the winner of 53 medals.

Gardens like this owed an enormous debt to the plant hunters. Their influence was particularly strong during the last years of the eighteenth century and the first decades of the nineteenth, when large numbers of new introductions were arriving in England from the Americas, South Africa, China, Australia and New Zealand.

A major role in promoting the search for new plants was played by the Royal Botanic Gardens at Kew, which had emerged as a leading force in the introduction and propagation of exotics during the latter part of the eighteenth century. After the death of Frederick Prince of Wales in 1751, his widow, Princess Augusta, who continued to live at Kew Palace, engaged the architect Sir William Chambers to improve the grounds and develop a small botanic garden. After her death in 1771, Kew benefited enormously from the appointment of Sir Joseph Banks as adviser. Banks had accompanied Captain Cook on his voyage round the world on the *Endeavour* from 1768 to 1771 and had returned with a considerable collection of botanical specimens and an awareness of the wealth of material waiting to be exploited in British possessions overseas. Through his contacts and the collectors he employed, many new

An autumn evening by the lake in the rhododendron ground at Biddulph, where the contrasting forms of deciduous trees and conifers bring variety to the planting.

plant introductions were made at Kew. Francis Masson brought heaths, pelargoniums, proteas, ixias, cinerarias and *Strelitzia regina* from South Africa and introduced 780 new plants in all. David Nelson travelled to Australia, Tasmania, the Cape and Timor, and is credited with the first eucalyptus, *Acacia verticillata, Cordyline australis, Phormium, Hypericum chinensis* and *Ranunculus nelsonii*. George Caley, who also collected in Australia, sent back the seeds of 170 new plants, including many species of eucalyptus.

After the death of Sir Joseph Banks in 1820 there was a decline at Kew until the appointment of Sir William Hooker, the Professor of Botany at Glasgow University, as first Director in 1841. He corresponded regularly with James Bateman, who received plants from Kew on numerous occasions. It was during Hooker's tenure of office that the herbarium was formed and the palm house and the Victoria Regia house were built. He was also editor from 1827 to 1844 of the *Botanical Magazine*, which had been founded by William Curtis in 1787 to illustrate and describe some of the most outstanding exotic plants cultivated in this country, both in the open ground and under glass. It continues today as the *Kew Magazine*.

Sir William Hooker's son, Joseph, who was to succeed him as Director at Kew, travelled to the Antarctic, New Zealand, Tasmania and India in search of new species. Many of the plants described in his *Rhododendrons of Sikkim-Himalaya* (1849–51) were introduced by him to European gardens, with Biddulph Grange an early beneficiary.

OPPOSITE PAGE *The rhododendron ground at Biddulph is at its best in May.*

LEFT *The palm house at Kew. James Bateman had close links with successive directors at the Royal Botanic Gardens, frequently receiving plants from them as well as sending plants to Kew from Biddulph.*

Tab. I.

J.D.H. del. Fitch, lith.

Reeve, Benham & Reeve, imp.

RHODODENDRON DALHOUSIÆ, Hook. fil.

(in its native locality)

W.Fitch, del.s. lith.

Vincent Brooks, Imp.

LEFT Rhododendron dalhousiae *in its native habitat, illustrated* *in Joseph Hooker's* Rhododendrons of Sikkim-Himalaya. *Bateman planted many of Joseph Hooker's introductions in the glen but later moved them to the rhododendron house, where* R. dalhousiae *flowered.*

ABOVE Rhododendron batemani, *named in honour of James Bateman by Dr Joseph Hooker, flowered at Biddulph Grange in 1863 and was then presented to Kew. The illustration is from* Curtis's Botanical Magazine.

23

No 1154

Pub by T. Curtis St Geo: Crefcent Nov 1. 1808.

Syd Edwards et. F. Sansom Sculp

Another important development for horticulture generally, and for the introduction of new plants in particular, was the founding of the Horticultural Society (later the Royal Horticultural Society) in 1804. John Wedgwood, son of Josiah, first proposed the formation of the society in a letter from Etruria Hall in the Potteries to William Forsyth, gardener to the King at the Royal Gardens, Kensington. The object of the Society, in Wedgwood's words, was 'to collect every information respecting the culture and treatment of all plants and trees, as well culinary as ornamental'. In due course the Horticultural Society became a considerable force through its publications, its garden for the cultivation and study of new plants, its shows and the work of the collectors it sent abroad. James Bateman was to play a prominent role in its activities and was to become a highly regarded vice-president. A key figure in the early history of the Society was John Lindley, who, as well as becoming its Secretary, was appointed Professor of Botany at University College, London, and Praefectus Horti of the Chelsea Physic Garden. His devotion to orchids brought him into frequent contact with Bateman.

One of the Society's correspondents overseas, John Reeves, worked in Canton and Macao as a tea inspector with the East India Company, and through him the Society received a number of azaleas, camellias, moutan peonies, roses and chrysanthemums, though many others were lost during the long and difficult journey. An expedition by George Don, brother of Patrick Don, who was head gardener at Knypersley in the 1830s, to Sierra Leone and the West Indies in 1821–2, yielded the guava, the Sierra Leone peach, the African locust tree, *Parkia africana* and other tropical fruits. In 1822–3 John Forbes sent back fine collections of plants from Brazil and East Africa before dying when still only twenty-three while travelling up the Zambezi. James McRae sailed in September 1824 to Brazil, the Hawaiian Islands, Chile and Peru and sent back many valuable seeds and plants, including the monkey puzzle, *Araucaria araucana*.

The most notable of the Society's collectors, and one who did more than any other to change the face of British gardens, was David Douglas. He was born in 1798, the son of a stonemason, and started his career as an apprentice gardener at Scone Palace. A later position at the Glasgow Botanic Garden brought him the acquaintance of William Hooker, who recommended him to Joseph Sabine, the Secretary of the Horticultural Society, as a botanical collector.

In 1823 he was sent to New York with the principal object of finding fruit trees to add to the Society's collection. His visits to orchards took him to Philadelphia and across the border into Canada, and he was given many specimens to take back to London. His descriptions of plants he had seen from the west coast of North America prompted the Horticultural Society to send him there the following year. After two weeks collecting orchids and other tropical plants in Rio de Janeiro and short stops at Juan Fernandez Island and at one of the Galapagos Islands, he reached the Columbia River. From there he

A moutan peony illustrated in Curtis's Botanical Magazine. Bateman prepared the most sheltered spot in 'China' for his moutan or tree peonies, but after ten disappointing years he was forced to move them to Knypersley where they flourished under glass.

Mountain hemlock, Tsuga mertensiana, *was introduced into England in 1854; it is seen here at Biddulph between a green and a golden yew.*

travelled for two years, by canoe, on horseback and on foot, often through country which had not previously been explored. He faced considerable danger and endured great hardship. Sometimes there was an abundance of food, some of it quite exotic, and a breakfast of bear and beaver might be followed by reindeer steaks for dinner. At other times he came near to starvation. After one particularly difficult day he wrote in his journal: 'travelled thirty-three miles, drenched and bleached with rain and sleet, chilled with a piercing north wind; and then to finish the day experienced the cooling, comfortless consolation of lying down wet without supper or fire. On such occasions I am very liable to become fretful.' But he saw many new things, among them *Mahonia aquifolium* and the great tree which the collector Archibald Menzies had found first in 1795 but which was to be known as the Douglas fir; and he brought back a great quantity of valuable plants and seeds.

David Douglas F.L.S. 1798-1834
enlarged from a pencil drawing ætat 30 by his niece Miss Atkinson

In 1829 he set out again, this time for California, but when he learned that Joseph Sabine had resigned as Secretary of the Society, he too resigned out of loyalty. It was a great loss to horticulture when he met his death in Honolulu after falling into a pit where, it seems, there was already a wild bull which gored him.

Among the plants introduced by Douglas were *Clarkia elegans*, *Limnanthes douglasii*, *Lupinus polyphyllus*, ancestor of modern lupins, *Garrya elliptica*, *Mimulus moschatus*, various penstemons and godetias, the Californian poppy, *Mahonia aquifolium*, the alpine *Douglasia*, *Ribes sanguineum*, *Pseudotsuga menziesii* (the Douglas fir), *Picea sitchensis* (the Sitka spruce), *Pinus lambertiana*, *P. ponderosa*, *P. sabiniana*, *P. coulteri*, *P. radiata*, *P. contorta*, *Abies grandis*, *A. nobilis*, *A. magnifica*, *A. douglasii* and *A. bracteata*. Most of them were to be found at Biddulph.

David Douglas, one of the greatest plant hunters, many of whose introductions from America were grown at Biddulph Grange.

27

TWO

The World's Greatest Nursery

Before setting off on his first visit to America in 1823 Douglas had gone to seek the advice of George Loddiges at the Hackney nursery, which, by this time, was probably overtaking Kew as the greatest collection of plants in the world. George's father, Conrad, was born in c.1738 in the village of Vristbergholtzen near Hildesheim in Hanover and served his apprenticeship in the gardens of George II in that kingdom. After working in Holland, he came to England in 1761 as gardener to Dr (later Sir) John Baptist Silvester in Hackney, and ten years later bought the nursery from a fellow Hanoverian, Johann Busch, when the latter was persuaded to go to St Petersburg to landscape gardens for Catherine the Great. Conrad Loddiges published his first catalogue in 1777 with plant names in Latin, German and English, and a foreword in German in which he stressed the care taken in packing plants to ensure that they travelled safely. In the 1783 catalogue there was a foreword in French as well as German as Loddiges continued to build up trade with the Continent.

The nursery was gradually extended until it covered fifteen well-planned acres, and Conrad was joined in the business by his sons, the outstandingly able and versatile George and his brother William. George was the father-in-law of Edward Cooke, who was to play such an important part at Biddulph, and it was mainly to him that Cooke owed his education as a gardener. George Loddiges was a member of the Council of the Horticultural Society from 1820 until his death in 1846 and, like Bateman, he was one of its vice-presidents and a fellow of the Linnean Society.

George Loddiges, the driving force in the Hackney nursery, an accomplished flower painter and father-in-law of Edward Cooke. Bateman placed Loddiges' nursery 'first on the list' among those 'who, by their zeal and skill, have brought orchis-growing to its present palmy state'.

In the Herbarium Library at Kew there is a list drawn up by William Loddiges of 151 plants which the nursery had introduced to general cultivation between 1782 and 1806. During the four decades which followed, this figure was to be multiplied many times. Between 1800 and 1818 the nursery supplied some 200 of the 1500 plants which were illustrated in the *Botanical Magazine*. In 1806 the then editor, John Simms, acknowledged the debt of British gardeners to Conrad Loddiges, who 'has been the means of introducing many rare exotics into our gardens', by naming a plant *Loddigesia oxalidifolia*. 'Linnaeus', he wrote, 'sometimes amused himself with fancying a resemblance between the

genus and the person to whose honour it is dedicated; and such conceits may at least serve to assist the memory. So in *Loddigesia*, the minute white standard may be considered as the emblem of the modest pretensions of this venerable cultivator; the broad keel, of his real usefulness to science; and the far-extended wings, as that of his two sons. *Sic praestent virtute patri, sic frugibus ambo*.*'

In 1817 the Loddiges began the publication of their own periodical, the *Botanical Cabinet*, which came out monthly for 16 years and was illustrated with a total of 2000 fine coloured plates of plants cultivated in the nursery. Most of them were drawn by George Loddiges and they were engraved by George Cooke, Edward's father. George Loddiges presumably also wrote the text accompanying each plate, which gives details of the place of origin of the plant illustrated, a brief description, cultural instructions and, in some cases, the circumstances of its discovery and introduction. Pious observations, mingled with the botanical and horticultural information, express the deeply held religious convictions of the author, who, as Edward Cooke wrote, 'looked through Nature to Nature's God'. 'Let us never, while we admire these engaging objects, forget that indulgent "Parent of Good", whose pencil paints them with such inimitable splendour.' George Loddiges looked forward (as did James Bateman) to the millennium, when 'the works of God will not always be so neglected as they have been, if as some suppose, we are drawing nearer to a period in which knowledge, peace and happiness will be perfected and extended beyond any thing that has yet been seen on earth'.

The Loddiges took a keen interest in the work of missionaries, a number of whom formed a valuable part of the nursery's world-wide network of correspondents and were responsible for sending many new plants to Hackney. Their horticultural contribution is gratefully acknowledged in the *Botanical Cabinet*, and their proselytising role warmly praised. 'Can anything be more glorious than to teach the ignorant and degraded pagans the ways of both temporal and everlasting happiness? . . . It is delightful in the present day to behold societies established for these benevolent purposes, and it proves that Britons do not undervalue the privileges which they enjoy, and are not so ungenerous as to deny their less favoured fellow creatures that sacred word of God, to which by his blessing they owe their own exalted distinction.'!

Other contacts were obtained through the nursery catalogue, in which the Loddiges invited those living in other parts of the world who shared their interest in plants to correspond with them. They were ready to pay a 'liberal price' for plants and seeds, but they also sought to exchange plants. They had this kind of arrangement with many of the leading gardens of Europe and made approaches to other bodies all over the world. Thus a report of the Wellington (New Zealand) Botanical Society for 1843 announces that their Secretary is in correspondence with Messrs Loddiges, who 'offer to send out boxes of whatever may be required from England, in exchange for the same

Loddigesia oxalidifolia, named in 1806 after Conrad Loddiges, the founder of the Hackney nursery; the illustration is from Curtis's Botanical Magazine.

* May they excel the father in virtue and in their achievements.

31

boxes full of native plants; more especially Coniferae, Orchideae and Ferns'. This was a more economical way of acquiring new plants than investing in a plant collector.

Many tributes were paid to the pre-eminence of the Hackney nursery in the 1820s and 1830s. A review of their catalogue which appeared in Loudon's *Gardener's Magazine* in 1826 praised every aspect of their enterprise: 'This Catalogue exhibits such an assemblage of plants, as, we will venture to assert, was never brought together by any individual, either in this country or abroad. The total number of species exceeds 8000, all plants that may be purchased, and exclusive of about 2000 varieties. In two departments, the superficial visitor will acknowledge the superiority of the Hackney garden; that of palms, and that of hardy trees and shrubs; the total number of species of the former at Hackney is 120, of the latter 2664. There is no such collection of hardy trees and shrubs in the world; and when it is considered that they may all enter our plantations, their value to the country is incalculable. In this department, Messrs Loddiges have done more than all the royal and botanic gardens put together.' George Johnson, whose *History of English Gardening* appeared in 1829, considered that the stock of the nursery (the value of which at retail prices he calculated to be £200,000) afforded 'a better criterion of the state of our Horticulture, and the efforts made to increase the number of our Garden Plants than any other I can make'.

The range of hothouses, with a total length of about a thousand feet, formed three sides of a rectangle. In the space they enclosed there were plants in pits and frames, beds for rare American and herbaceous plants and a section of plants for sale in pots. The hothouses were heated by steam, as was George Loudon's house, from one large boiler. Jacob Rinz, a nurseryman from Frankfurt-on-Main, wrote in the *Gardener's Magazine* about his visit to the nursery in 1829: 'The first garden that I visited was that of Messrs Loddiges, and never shall I forget the sensation produced in me by that establishment. I cannot describe the raptures I experienced on seeing that immense palm house. I fancied myself in the Brazils; and especially at that moment when Mr Loddiges had the kindness to produce, in my presence, a shower of artificial rain. Under such natural and perfect management, the palms, ferns and other plants, appeared just as might be expected. I was surprised at the vast ranges of green-houses and hot-houses; particularly at the beautiful curvilinear camellia house, in which the plants produced the most beautiful effect.' (The camellia house, measuring 120 feet long, 23 feet wide and 18 feet high, was erected in 1821 by Bailey of Holborn.) The artificial rain was contrived by means of a perforated half-inch lead pipe running under the roof and linked to an elevated cistern. Another visitor from the Continent in the 1820s wrote: 'We have met with no stoves, belonging to prince, king, or emperor, which can compare with those of Messrs Loddiges at Hackney, for the magnificence, convenience and elegance of their plan, and the value of their contents.'

LODDIGE'S PALMARUM.

The palm house at Loddiges' nursery, where James Bateman was a frequent visitor. Their 1845 palm catalogue listed 264 varieties, and a surviving copy is marked with prices ranging from £1 to £300. The illustration is from the Pictorial Times.

A notable display garden, covering about nine acres and called the Arboretum, was planted with trees and shrubs arranged in alphabetical order along a carefully-planned network of walks. One well-grown labelled specimen of each species or variety was followed by a stock of smaller plants which could be purchased. A remarkable variety was available. In 1836, for example, Loddiges listed in their catalogue 67 species and varieties of oak, 29 of birch, 91 of thorns, 180 of willow and a staggering 1549 roses. At the heart of the garden a series of concentric grass paths alternating with beds of peat housed a large collection of American plants.

The range of available stock continued to increase in the early 1840s – 1900 species of orchids were available in 1844 – but there was a decline after the deaths of George Loddiges in 1846 and of William three years later. In 1850 George's son Conrad wrote to a customer: 'We are sorry to say the taste for *botanical* plants has much degenerated of late.' A large part of the land occupied by the nursery belonged to St Thomas's Hospital, and since the lease was coming to an end, Conrad decided to cease trading and arranged for J. C. Stevens, the auctioneer, to sell all the stock in a series of auctions. This was announced by Stevens in an advertisement in the *Gardeners' Chronicle* on 22 May 1852, and a sale of hardy conifers in pots followed three days later at 38 King Street, Covent Garden. A first sale of orchids was held shortly afterwards, but then Sir Joseph Paxton* stepped in and bought all the remaining stock for the Crystal Palace Company, which he had formed to move the Crystal Palace from Hyde Park to Sydenham in Kent.

Among the plants to be moved from Hackney to Sydenham was the great collection of palms, comprising almost 300 species. William Loddiges had tried in vain to sell them to Kew in 1846, suggesting a price of £9000, 'vastly below the true value', and four years later an approach from Conrad, prepared to accept 'a much lower price', also failed to interest Sir William Hooker. In 1851 some of the palms were moved temporarily to Hyde Park for the Great Exhibition, and on 25 April Edward Cooke wrote in his diary: 'Went early to the Exhibition, assisted Conrad in arranging his Palms.'

It took some time to move the stock from the nursery to Sydenham. The giant among the plants at Hackney was the fan palm of Mauritius, *Latania borbonica*, which had once been in the collection of the Empress Josephine at Fontainebleau. Moving large trees had become a fairly common practice – some were moved at Biddulph – but it was a considerable feat to move this particular tree to Sydenham, and when it was safely delivered the carrier sat down and wrote a letter to *The Times*:

Sir, Yesterday we undertook to remove the celebrated palmtree from Mr Lodge's [sic], Hackney, to the Crystal Palace. The root was enclosed in a strong box about 12 feet square, bound with strong iron hoops weighing 15 cwt. The height of the plant

* See pp. 34–6.

Moving the palm Latania borbonica *from Loddiges' nursery at Hackney to the Crystal Palace at Sydenham. The Victorians, including James Bateman, enjoyed the challenge of moving large trees. The palm is here seen crossing London Bridge, with the Tower of London visible in the distance. 'The progress of this stupendous tree through the metropolis . . . will not be easily forgotten' (Illustrated London News).*

was about 30 feet. It was placed on a strong-built carriage that weighed upwards of 7 tons. The weight of the whole was upwards of 20 tons. There were 20 horses put to the trunk to move it from the place where it had been for more than 30 years. At the foot of Sydenham-hill there was a relay of 30 horses to take it up. It was taken through the streets and over London-bridge without any accident; the crowd being so great, it frequently had to stop. It was safely lodged at the Palace about 9 o'clock.

Yours respectfully
T. Younghusband
Gerards-hall-inn, 23 Old Bailey, July 28 [1854]

Shortly afterwards, on 17 August, Edward Cooke attended a final sale at the nursery when hothouses, conservatories, 1,000,000 bricks and other materials and equipment were disposed of. Conrad Loddiges probably continued to live in the house at the entrance, which had once been the home of William Loddiges, and he may have kept some of the hothouses, for in September 1856 he gave 174 orchids to Kew and a few more two years later.

Nothing now remains of the once great Hackney nursery, the site of which lies buried between Mare Street and Chatham Place, but for more than half a century it was a major force in world horticulture. While we have few records of Bateman's purchases of plants, he had considerable contact with George Loddiges, whom he greatly admired, and it seems certain that many specimens from the nursery found their way to Knypersley and Biddulph.

The development of the Loddiges' extensive range of hothouses reflected a general increase in the use of glass to provide the right conditions for plants from warmer climates. 'A green-house, which fifty years ago was a luxury not often to be met with,' wrote Loudon in *The Greenhouse Companion* in 1824, 'is now become an appendage to every villa, and to many town residences.' Although Loddiges' hothouses were thought incomparable in the 1820s, they were soon to be surpassed by those devised by Joseph Paxton for the 6th Duke of Devonshire. The son of a Bedfordshire farmer, Paxton had impressed the

Duke when he was working in the Chiswick Garden (adjacent to the Duke's seat at Chiswick House and leased by him to the Horticultural Society) and it was a master-stroke to appoint him head gardener at Chatsworth at the age of twenty-three. Under Paxton's influence plants and gardening became a consuming interest of the Duke's – he was President of the Horticultural Society from 1838 until his death in 1858 – while Paxton enjoyed a brilliant career as cultivator, landscaper, administrator, architect, entrepreneur and member of parliament.

After a number of earlier essays in the construction of glass buildings Paxton designed and constructed the Great Stove at Chatsworth between 1836 and 1840. It was the largest glass building in the world, 277 feet long, 123 feet wide

When the Great Stove at Chatsworth was completed, Bateman sent the 6th Duke of Devonshire some tropical fruit trees which had outgrown their hothouse at Knypersley.

and 67 feet high, covering an acre. Flights of steps under rustic arches, with overhanging blocks of gritstone covered with orchids, ferns, cactuses and creeping plants, led to a gallery running round the base of a dome from which the exotic landscape could be viewed. 'From the smallest aquatic plants down to the most stately palms, and from the banana down to the papyrus and the delicate ferns, every conceivable rarity is here, flourishing in native luxuriance and endless profusion' (Black's *Tourist Guide to Derbyshire*). One could drive through it in a carriage and pair, as Queen Victoria and Prince Albert did in 1843, when it was lit by 20,000 lamps of various colours. 'After St Peter's there is nothing like the Conservatory', was the Duchess of Sutherland's verdict, though another visitor was reminded only of an ethnic garden in Jamaica.

In 1849 Paxton designed a house for the giant water-lily *Victoria amazonica* (formerly called *Victoria regia*), which he had flowered at Chatsworth for the first time the previous year. His culminating triumph in glass came two years later with the construction of the Crystal Palace in Hyde Park. This innovative building covered 19 acres and earned him his knighthood.

New plants for England's greenhouses and gardens were arriving in ever increasing numbers, but many more were perishing during the journey. Plants conveyed by sea fell into two categories – the few which were kept in a passive state and the majority which had to be kept growing during the voyage. Loddiges recommended that the former should be packed between layers of sphagnum moss, except cactuses and succulents for which the driest sand should be used. Plants which had to be kept growing were much more difficult, and very many succumbed to variations of temperature, to the failure to water correctly, to sea spray or to lack of light. It was not unusual for whole consignments of plants to be lost. Seeds were an alternative to plants, but the difficulties in raising exotic plants from seed very often defeated those who tried.

This situation was to be changed by a friend of George Loddiges and a frequent visitor to the nursery, Nathaniel Ward, the son of a medical practitioner in Wellclose Square near to London's docks. His early interest in natural history was fostered by a visit at the age of thirteen to Jamaica, where he was deeply impressed by the tropical vegetation, particularly the palms and the ferns.

While Ward succeeded his father in the practice at Wellclose Square and performed his duties there with great diligence, dawn expeditions to botanise on Shooter's Hill or Wimbledon Common and frequent evening visits to Kew, the Hackney nursery or the Chelsea Physic Garden reflected his continuing commitment to natural history and horticulture. In his small garden he made even more spectacular use of limited space than did Loudon in Porchester Terrace. Plants grew in boxes and troughs along the tops of walls, there were boxes of plants in every window, while even the roofs of sheds were covered in soil and planted.

One day in 1829 he brought home the chrysalis of a hawk-moth and placed it to develop in some moist earth in a large bottle with a lid. This it did about a month afterwards, when Ward also noticed two tiny green shoots appearing through the soil and placed the bottle in a north-facing window to see what would happen. The plants turned out to be a fern and a grass and they continued to live in the bottle for three years without being watered and without the lid being removed. Both finally died when the lid rusted and rain-water got in.

Ward repeated this experiment with similar results with more than sixty species of ferns and with some other plants, many of them provided for the purpose by George Loddiges. They were placed in a moistened mixture of bog-moss, vegetable mould and sand in near-airtight boxes with glass lids and sides. He found that ferns and some other plants could then grow for years without a fresh supply of water, for the amount of moisture in the cases remained constant. Ward realised that such cases had great potential for transporting plants. He saw, too, that plants in enclosed cases were protected from polluted air, and that there were other possible applications, such as in the germination of seeds. He later acknowledged his debt to Loddiges: 'To the Messrs Loddiges, who may most justly be styled "*Hortularum Principes*", the

A Wardian case used to transport plants on long sea voyages, one of Edward Cooke's illustrations for Nathaniel Ward's On the Growth of Plants in Closely Glazed Cases *(1852).*

thanks of the author are most especially due. From the very commencement of his enquiries their splendid stoves were placed unreservedly at his disposal, and without their kind assistance it would have been difficult for him to have carried on his experiments.'

In June 1833 he sent two cases containing ferns and other plants to Sydney, Australia. At least some of the plants – probably all of them – were again provided by Loddiges, and it seems safe to assume that the cases were filled at Hackney. The plants arrived safely, and the cases were refilled with other plants for the return journey. They passed through temperatures ranging from 20° to 120°F and were not watered, but when Ward and Loddiges went to inspect them they found them in excellent condition. 'I will not readily forget', wrote Ward, 'the delight expressed by Mr. G. Loddiges, who accompanied me on board, at the beautiful appearance of *Gleichenia microphylla*, a plant now seen for the first time alive in this country.'

Loddiges at once began to use Wardian cases for conveying plants to and from all parts of the world, and the 6th Duke of Devonshire's promising young gardener, John Gibson, went to Hackney to discuss them before using them in India. Gibson's expedition was very successful and more than 300 fine plants, including *Amherstia nobilis*, reached Chatsworth.

The Duke had been particularly anxious to obtain the *Amherstia*, a sacred tree of great beauty, his interest having been aroused by a letter from the Revd J. T. Huntley, a leading orchid grower, in which the latter quoted from the journal of the plant collector George Finlayson: 'Nothing in the vegetable World could exceed in Beauty the Appearance of this stately Plant as it stood erect on the Stem of an aged Tree, surrounded by its flowering leaves, rather resembling the Frond of a Palm than the Leaf of an herbaceous Plant. The flowering Spike alone exceeded six Feet in length, containing nearly one hundred Flowers, & was now in full blossom. The flowers exhaled a most grateful but mild odour; they were about two inches and a half across, & upwards of four including the footstalk, in length. The Petals are waived on the Margin, of a fleshy consistence, of a dark yellow colour interspersed with iron brown spots.'

Nathaniel Wallich, the Danish-born Superintendent of the Calcutta Botanic Garden, gave Gibson two plants of the *Amherstia*, one for the Duke of Devonshire and one for the Court of Directors of the Honourable East India Company. Unfortunately, the plant addressed to the Duke died during the journey. Gibson wrote to the Duke suggesting that he should write to the Company and ask for the surviving plant 'as you have the greater claim upon it'. The Court of Directors could then have a plant as soon as it could be propagated. The Duke followed his young gardener's advice and the Directors readily agreed to the request. Paxton, in a letter from Chatsworth to the Duke at his Chiswick seat, had had no doubts about what he would do. 'If ever I put my hands on *Amherstia*, all the Directors in the world shall never make me let go of it till it reaches Chatsworth.'

Amherstia nobilis, introduced by John Gibson to Chatsworth in 1835, where it failed to flower. Bateman explained why in a lecture to the Horticultural Society some thirty years later, identifying the kyanised tub in which it was planted as the cause of the trouble. The illustration is from Curtis's Botanical Magazine.

Fitch, del et lith.

R B & R. imp.

Once the *Amherstia* was in Paxton's hands all that remained was to get it to flower. But the plant struggled even to survive, and the success which eluded the Duke was not achieved until twelve years later, when that great gardener Mrs Louisa Lawrence was able to present a bouquet of flowers from her *Amherstia* to Queen Victoria. Bateman explained what had gone wrong in a lecture to the Royal Horticultural Society on 27 March 1866. A house had been specially prepared at Chatsworth to receive the plant, but it was put into a tub which had been kyanised, and this was the cause of the trouble. The process of kyanising was a new way of preserving wood, introduced by a certain J. H. Kyan, and it was some time before it was realised that the substance used was harmful to growing plants.

In his philanthropy Nathaniel Ward had hoped that his cases would prove a boon to the poorer classes, living in smoke-filled cities, who would be able to enjoy the pleasures of horticulture. The small capital outlay would soon be defrayed by growing salads and radishes for the table. Just before he died, in his seventy-seventh year, he was working on ideas for improving the dwellings of the poor both through his cases and in other ways; but it was in the 'homes of taste' of the Victorian bourgeoisie that the Wardian case made its mark. Ward's simple utilitarian prototypes on his window-sills in Wellclose Square developed through the substantial but restrained free-standing examples, for which plans were provided in the *Gardener's Magazine*, to a wide range of increasingly elaborate and sometimes rather monstrous models which were set pieces and often the centre pieces in parlours and drawing-rooms for several decades. In the second edition of his book *On the Growth of Plants in Closely Glazed Cases* (1852), Ward illustrates his Tintern Abbey case 'containing in the centre a small model in pumice and Bath stone of the West window of Tintern Abbey'. The sides were built of rock-work to a height of about five feet and a perforated pipe provided artificial rain as in the hothouses at Hackney. The drawings illustrating this and other cases were by Edward Cooke and his sister, Georgiana, married to Nathaniel Ward's son, Stephen.

The Victorian fern craze developed hand in hand with the Wardian case, though there was already an increasing interest in ferns before the latter was introduced, for they combined very well with the rock-work, root-work and rustic elements which were then becoming popular in gardens. Articles on the cultivation of ferns appeared in the 1820s in the *Transactions of the Horticultural Society* and in the *Gardener's Magazine*, and many species were being cultivated by Loddiges, by the Liverpool Botanic Garden and by Robert Barclay, a leading amateur with a large garden at Bury Hill in Surrey. Numerous books devoted to ferns started appearing in the late 1830s, one of the most successful being Thomas Moore's *A Popular History of the British Ferns*, dedicated to Nathaniel Ward. Much of the appeal of this work lay in the lists of places where the less common species could be found, since rambling for ferns had become a popular pastime. Fern collecting by the few had been harmless enough, but

when it became a mass activity with large-scale commercial participation it began to threaten the continued existence of some species, at least in some locations, as amateurs advanced with trowels and hampers and dealers with spades and carts.

After Ward had retired he moved to Clapham Rise, where he again devoted himself to his small garden, his glazed cases, his herbarium and a fernery. When Dr Fisher, the Director of the Imperial Botanic Garden in St Petersburg, visited him there and saw the fern *Trichmanes speciosum* growing in one of Ward's cases, he took off his hat, bowed to the plant and congratulated Ward on succeeding where he had failed. The fernery was designed by Edward Cooke, without ventilation like a Wardian case, though it was shaded from the sun in hot weather. Guided by his memories of Jamaica, Ward sought to recreate in it a tropical forest, with palms, ferns, bamboos, bananas, passion-flowers, manettias, aristolochias, cannas and clerodendrons picturesquely arranged.

He frequently entertained those who shared his interests and Sir Joseph Hooker wrote of him: 'During the whole period that I knew him and I believe for many years before, his hospitable house, first in Wellclose Square, and latterly at Clapham Rise, was the most frequented metropolitan resort of naturalists from all quarters of the globe of any since Sir Joseph Banks. . . . Of the value of that contrivance, which justly bears his name, the Ward's case, it is impossible to speak too strongly; and I feel safe in saying that a large proportion of the most valuable economic and other tropical plants now cultivated in

Edward Cooke designed the fern house at Clapham Rise for Nathaniel Ward, who wished to create a scene reminiscent of the tropical forest he had seen in Jamaica in his youth.

OPPOSITE PAGE *These Wardian cases, drawn by Edward Cooke and intended to contain ferns and other plants for ornamental use, were probably designed by Cooke for the Great Exhibition of 1851, where he and his friend Ward showed cases to the public. On 2 June he 'went at half p 8 to the Exhibition, to receive the Queen and explain the Fern cases, but she did not visit my stand.'*

England would, but for these cases, not yet have been introduced.'

Certainly many of the plants at Biddulph owed their presence in part to Nathaniel Ward, particularly those which were introduced by the Scotsman Robert Fortune, the Horticultural Society's collector in China appointed in 1843 and the first to visit China with the benefit of Wardian cases. In spite of the transport difficulties there had already been some notable introductions from China, among them azaleas, camellias, chrysanthemums and tree peonies, but because of the tight restrictions on foreigners it had for some time seemed hardly worthwhile to send collectors there. Fortune's appointment had been prompted by the Treaty of Nanking (1842), concluding the Opium War (1839–42), which resulted in the ceding of Hong Kong and the opening of additional ports to British trade.

Before he left Fortune was given lengthy written instructions. He was 'to collect seeds and plants of an ornamental or useful kind, not already cultivated in Great Britain, and to obtain information upon Chinese gardening and agriculture together with the nature of their climate and its apparent influence upon vegetation'. Among the plants the Society was particularly anxious to acquire were tea plants, the peaches cultivated in the Emperor's garden – each of which was said to weigh two pounds – double yellow roses, blue peonies 'the existence of which is, however, doubtful' and yellow camellias. Wherever possible Fortune was to send sufficient seed for distribution to members of the Society, and he was to collect samples of soils, especially the soils in which camellias, chrysanthemums and azaleas did best. Fortune took with him a quantity of seeds and three Wardian cases filled with plants, partly to see how the latter responded but also to give as presents in return for favours.

Although the restrictions were by then a little less vigorous, it was still very difficult for a foreigner to travel easily in China, but Fortune was very resourceful and succeeded in disguising himself successfully as a Chinese on a number of occasions. He was particularly pleased when the dogs failed to spot him as an impostor! From Hong Kong he travelled first to Amoy, then to Chusan, Shanghai and eventually Suchow, where in one of the nurseries he found 'a white *Glycine* [wistaria], a fine new double yellow rose, and a *Gardenia* with white blossoms, like a Camellia. These plants are now in England, and will soon be met with in every garden in the country'. He also visited the Fa Tee nurseries in Canton, which had already been an important source of plants for European visitors, and it is probable that Fortune, too, bought many plants there. The plants were arranged in pots along narrow paved walks in about twelve separate gardens. Fortune found the nurseries at their best in spring: 'They are then gay with the tree peony, azaleas, camellias, roses, and various other plants. The azaleas are splendid and reminded me of the exhibitions in the gardens of the Horticultural Society in Chiswick, but the Fa-tee exhibitions are on a much larger scale. Every garden was one mass of bloom, and the different colours of red, white and purple, blended together, had a most beautiful and

Plants introduced by Robert Fortune from China and Japan were a major contribution to the garden at Biddulph Grange.

42

composing effect. . . . The air at this season is perfumed with the sweet flowers of *Olea fragrans* and the *Magnolia fuscata*, both of which are extensively grown in these gardens.' (In 1981, during a visit to Canton, members of the Garden History Society succeeded in finding what appeared to be these same nurseries which a century and a half ago were supplying plants destined for English gardens.)

Among the many plants which reached England from Fortune's first expedition to the Far East were *Cryptomeria japonica*, *Jasminum nudiflorum*, *Viburnum macrocephalum*, *Viburnum tomentosum*, *Dicentra spectabilis*, *Forsythia viridissima*, *Weigela florida*, numerous varieties of tree peony and a few chrysanthemums.

After his return to England Fortune was appointed Curator of the Chelsea Physic Garden, but in 1848 the East India Company approached him to go back to China to obtain a considerable quantity of tea plants for shipment to India for plantations in Sikkim and Assam. This was a very difficult undertaking, and he again travelled at times in Chinese costume. In his first year he was able to send a considerable amount of seed, but tea seed does not remain viable for long and hardly any of it germinated. In the following year he sowed

The Fa Tee nursery, Canton, in 1981. Fortune visited the Fa Tee nursery and probably bought plants there, some of which may have reached Biddulph.

Weigela florida, introduced by Robert Fortune, flowers in 'China' in May and June.

it in Wardian cases before sending it. This proved successful and he sent many more plants and seeds in the third year. Among the plants Fortune discovered during this expedition was *Mahonia bealii*. 'The shrub was about eight feet high, much branched, and far surpassed in beauty all the other known species of Mahonia.' He was able to send three specimens back to England.

His work in China and in India had benefited enormously from the use of Wardian cases and he wrote to Ward to acknowledge his debt: 'We have done wonders with your cases in India as well as in this country. . . . When I tell you that nearly twenty thousand tea-plants were taken in *safety* and in *high health* from Shanghae to the Himalayas, you will have an idea of our success. The same success attended some cases packed by me for the United States. A large number of rare and beautiful trees and shrubs sent by me at different times to this country have arrived in the best order – scarcely a species has been lost. For these results we are indebted to you.'

44

The plants introduced by Fortune made a considerable contribution to Biddulph Grange, and Bateman must have followed the progress of these journeys to China with the same keen interest he had taken in earlier expeditions to South and Central America. The main object of those expeditions had been orchids.

In the history of horticulture there are one or two plants which have been valued above all others. One is the tulip, which became the object of wild speculation in seventeenth-century Holland with fortunes being won and lost and huge sums paid for single bulbs of new sports. Some varieties of tulip continued to be highly valued in England two centuries later – prices quoted in 1839 ranged from two shillings for *Georgius Tertius* to £50 for *Groom's William IV* – but by the second half of the century orchids had come to be esteemed above all other flowers and were often sold for prices which only the richest could pay.

The first tropical orchid to flower in England – *Bletia purpurea** in 1731 – had been sent from the Bahamas to Peter Collinson, a wholesale woollen draper and distinguished botanist. It was forty years before a second success was recorded, this time a plant of *Phaius grandifolius*, imported from China by Dr John Fothergill, medical practitioner, botanist and gardener. At the end of the century there were still only a few species of orchids in the Royal Botanic Gardens at Kew. Loddiges' nursery, around 1812, seems to have been the first to cultivate them commercially and in 1831 they were able to offer over 300 species, a figure which had risen to 1600 when they published their first orchid catalogue in 1839. James Bateman was prominent among early private collectors, who also included Mrs Louisa Lawrence, the 6th Duke of Devonshire and Bateman's friend, the Revd J. T. Huntley.

A list of orchids and a guide to prices were given in *Paxton's Magazine of Botany* in 1835. The commoner kinds were said to be available at prices ranging from ten shillings to £10 each from Loddiges of Hackney, Low of Clapton, Knight of Chelsea and Rollisson of Tooting, 'though some seem scarcely to be met with at any price, except in private collections'. As orchidomania developed later in the century, single specimens not infrequently changed hands for several hundreds of pounds, and there were regular sales of orchids in London by the auctioneers Protheroe and Morris in Cheapside and Stevens in Covent Garden, which were always well attended by the leading collectors and nurserymen.

Orchids were big business and the high prices paid led to ruthless practices. There was often intense rivalry between collectors for different firms who found themselves working the same territory, and extreme measures were sometimes adopted in order to frustrate competitors. Worst of all was the total destruction of all remaining orchids once a collector had secured what he could carry away. Dirty tricks apart, the sheer volume of trade carried a grave threat

*The names of all orchids referred to in the text are those used in the nineteenth century.

An orchid collector at work. James Bateman was still a student at Oxford when he sent Thomas Colley to collect orchids for him in British Guiana.

to habitats in all areas where plants were intensively gathered without any thought for conservation. Messrs William Bull, in May 1878, announced that they had received two consignments totalling an estimated 2,000,000 orchids, while Benedict Roezl once sent 8 tons of orchids in a single shipment. Alfred Millican, in *Travels and Adventures of an Orchid Hunter*, described one of the many sites in Colombia which had been ravaged by collectors: 'On the ledges of these precipices, where the eagle and the condor make their home, the lovely *Cattleya Mendelii* has grown in profusion since the memory of man. When the first plant-hunter arrived, these dizzy heights offered no obstacle to his determination to plunder. Natives were let down by means of ropes, and by the same ropes the plants were hauled up in thousands, and when I visited the place all that I could see of its former beauty and wealth of plants was an occasional struggling bulb hung as if in mid-air only accessible to eagles.' It was not only orchids which suffered, for sometimes vast tracts of forest were clear-felled in order to gather the epiphytic species from the upper branches.

Sadly many species were lost through the activities of the orchid hunters, for after their native habitats had been stripped the plants perished in the greenhouses of Europe through lack of skill in their cultivation.

It was not unusual for collectors of orchids also to collect humming-birds, for the two were found together in the wild, were equally spectacular and were frequently sent back together from South and Central America. George Loddiges was particularly devoted to the study of humming-birds, and his collection was renowned throughout Europe. It was his unrealised intention to illustrate them in a folio volume. The British Museum acquired his collection from a descendant in 1933 along with his catalogue and notes. Prices for humming-birds were comparable with those paid for orchids. The entry in Jane Loddiges's diary on 22 January 1840 reads: 'My Uncle William presented Papa with a blue-tailed humming bird which cost 20 guineas – the only one besides Mr Leadbeater's in the country.' James Bateman also had a collection of humming-birds in the museum at Biddulph Grange.

To collect and cultivate orchids, to stock a private museum and to create a remarkable garden required not only great skill and dedication but also considerable means. James Bateman was fortunate that his family circumstances enabled him to indulge his enthusiasms and to develop his talents.

Orchid collectors were often equally attracted to humming-birds, which were found in similar habitats; there was a collection of humming-birds in the museum at Biddulph Grange.

THREE

Two Eminent Victorians

By the 1840s, through the dedication of Loudon, the Loddiges, Ward, Douglas, Fortune and others, there was a great wealth of new ideas and new material for the makers of gardens. None was to use them more effectively than James Bateman and Edward Cooke at Biddulph Grange. Both had considerable talents and they shared many intellectual interests, while their early careers had prepared them well for the task of creating an exceptional garden.

James Bateman was born at Redivals near Bury in Lancashire, the home of his mother's family, in 1811, but his parents, John and Elizabeth Bateman, moved to Knypersley Hall in Staffordshire, and he was brought up there. John's father, another James, had bought the Knypersley and adjacent Biddulph Vicarage estates in 1810, and it was he who had built up the family's considerable fortune. He was born at Tolson Hall, near Kendal in Westmorland, in 1749. As a young man he was impressed by his father's acquaintances' successful careers in industry and decided that this was where his future lay. One of his father's friends, Christopher Wilson, a banker in Kendal, had a nephew who was an ironmonger in Manchester, and James Bateman went to join him with the possibility of taking over the business. Shortly afterwards he bought out Wilson's stock with £4000 advanced by his father on the understanding that the remainder of the estate would be inherited by James's younger brother. The business prospered, and he built an iron foundry and a mill for drawing wire, acquired an interest in an iron furnace and collieries at Dukinfield in Cheshire and in ironworks at Acton Bridge in Cheshire and in Liverpool. He became the largest importer of Swedish and Russian iron in the country.

In the 1780s Bateman formed a partnership with a gifted engineer, William Sherratt, and together they developed an extensive ironworks in Salford, where, as manufacturers of steam-engines, they became fierce competitors of Matthew Boulton and James Watt of Soho near Birmingham. In 1796 they had to pay substantial damages for infringing the latters' patents. They also made steam-engines, boilers and a wide range of other iron products at a factory at Shelton in the Potteries.

James Bateman (1811–97),
who with the help of
Edward Cooke (1811–80)
designed both the house and
the garden at Biddulph
Grange.

Bateman's interests were not confined to iron and coal. He also built three large cotton-mills in Manchester and a range of warehouses known as Bateman's Buildings, and towards the end of his career, as we know from a letter written by his son, he 'joined the Banking house of his friend Mr Wilson, the interests of which he greatly contributed to'. He spent the last years of his life in his native Westmorland.

The estates at Knypersley and Biddulph were bought for their mineral and industrial potential. There were abundant reserves of coal, and Bateman thought that he might establish furnaces there in conjunction with his ironworks in Manchester. A number of small coal-mines already being worked in the eighteenth century were further developed by the Batemans, in particular the Childerplay Colliery, later known as Victoria Pit. In 1857 this was leased to the great iron and coal master, Robert Heath (who was later to acquire Biddulph Grange), under whom it prospered.

But James Bateman's heirs were more interested in country pursuits than industrial enterprises. Game and gardens appealed more than coal and iron, and, thanks to him, they could afford to follow their inclinations. Knypersley Hall was a pleasant, substantial house, set in extensive grounds and parkland and surrounded by fine countryside, which was not yet spoilt by industrial activity. John Bateman played a leading role in the community, maintaining the fabric of St Lawrence's Church, Biddulph, of which he was patron, building a new school and church – St John the Evangelist – in Knypersley, furthering the interests of the Tory party and its local mouthpiece, the

A stained-glass window (c.1896) at Biddulph Grange shows a scene from a coal mine by an unknown artist. Biddulph Grange was founded on the profits from coal by the Batemans and maintained by them under the Heaths.

Staffordshire Gazette, helping to finance the toll road which improved communications between the Potteries and Manchester, supplying soup to those in need in times of unemployment, and serving as High Sheriff of Staffordshire and as patron of local learned and philanthropic societies. He and Elizabeth were both interested in gardening and in 1832 they sought the help of Thomas Trubshaw, architect and landscape gardener, paying him ten guineas for 'attending many times at Knypersley, consulting respecting Flower Garden and making several elaborate coloured Plans for the same'. They each ordered plants from Caldwell's nursery, still flourishing in Knutsford, and lists of the plants they ordered have survived in Caldwell's day book for 1834 in the Cheshire County Record Office. They helped to foster a love of flowers and gardening in their son James.

This enthusiasm began with orchids, 'the master passion of his life', which was to bring him international fame. 'I was devoted to orchids long before I knew what an orchid was, indeed, the word itself was quite strange to me when I heard my mother apply it to a beautiful plant with spotted leaves and speckled flowers which I had gathered in a country lane and regarded with great admiration. "That," she said, "is an orchis".' James was about eight years old at the time. Ten years later, when he was a student at Magdalen College, Oxford, he visited Thomas Fairburn's nursery on the site now occupied by Keble College. 'This sealed my fate!' Fairburn, who had previously been gardener to Sir Joseph Banks and Prince Leopold (later King of the Belgians), drew James's attention to a curious plant with leathery leaves and stout roots and then opened the pages of the *Botanical Magazine* to show him the drawing of the Chinese air plant, *Renanthera coccinea*, as it had flowered in Prince Leopold's garden at Bushey Park in Hertfordshire and from which he had taken the cutting. 'Of course I fell in love at first sight, and as Mr Fairburn asked only a guinea for his plant (high prices were not yet in vogue) it soon changed hands and travelled with me to Knypersley, when the Christmas holidays began. I had caught my first Orchid, but how to treat it I knew not.' It seems that he was so charmed by the treasures of the nursery that he remained there when he should have been in college and was required by its vice-president, Dr Daubeny (later Professor of Botany), to write out half the Book of Psalms.

Bateman soon succumbed to orchidomania and built up a collection of orchids at Knypersley. After his first meeting in Hackney in 1832 with George Loddiges, whom he found in his studio drawing an orchid for the *Botanical Cabinet*, Bateman was to see him frequently at the nursery and at meetings of the Horticultural Society. He had the greatest admiration for Loddiges and wrote of him with deep affection years afterwards: 'His devotion to Orchids and humming birds was intense but though he loved the birds beyond the plants, yet I doubt whether any man ever loved the plants so much as he.' It was probably Loddiges who introduced him to humming-birds. In 1833, while still a student at Magdalen, he sent, with his father's encouragement, a plant

OVERLEAF LEFT *James Bateman bought his first orchid when he was a student at Magdalen College, Oxford, after a nurseryman in the town had shown him this illustration of* Renanthera coccinea *in* Curtis's Botanical Magazine. *'It soon changed hands and travelled with me to Knypersley, when the Christmas holidays began.'*

OVERLEAF RIGHT Oncidium lanceanum: *Thomas Colley brought back specimens of this orchid from British Guiana for Bateman in 1834, and everyone was 'prepared to go down on their knees for a bit, offering their greatest treasures in exchange'. The illustration appeared in the* Transactions of the Horticultural Society.

W.J.H.delt.

Pub. by S.Curtis Walworth. July. 1.1830.

's Drake. del.

Oncidium Lanceanum?

George Ure Skinner, who was persuaded by Bateman to collect orchids in Guatemala.

collector to British Guiana to search for orchids. The man Bateman engaged was Thomas Colley, Thomas Fairburn's foreman. He sent back some sixty different kinds of orchid, about a third of them new, and while they were generally unremarkable, they included *Oncidium lanceanum*, which had 'made collectors mad' when it was first discovered in Surinam by James Bateman's acquaintance the barrister J. H. Lance. Colley found a tree covered with this species and, knowing that Francis Henchman, a collector working for Low's nursery in Clapton, was only a day and a half behind him, 'he immediately set to work and stripped the tree, determined not to give the others a chance'. Bateman added, without apparent regret: 'Nor, so far as I know, has the species ever been found before or since in that country.' As soon as it was known that he had plants of this particular species, everyone was 'prepared to go down on their knees for a bit, offering their greatest treasures in exchange'.

Another source of orchids was George Ure Skinner, the son of a Scottish clergyman, who had a trading company in Guatemala. John Gould, the ornithologist, persuaded him to take an interest in the birds of the country, and when Bateman saw some specimens sent to the Museum of Natural History in Manchester, he wrote to Skinner to encourage him to look for orchids. Skinner responded enthusiastically, not only collecting them himself but employing others to collect them for him.

It was not long before Bateman received his first carefully packed consignment and he was delighted to find that every plant was new. At Bateman's request Dr Lindley named one of them *Barkeria skinneri*. Another, *Odontoglossum bictoniense*, was the first living example of that genus to reach England. *Odontoglossum uro-skinneri*, *Cattleya skinneri* and, most notably, *Lycaste skinneri* were among many more discoveries which were to follow.

In 1866, at the age of sixty-two, Skinner set out on his twentieth and last journey to Guatemala before retiring. On 26 December he was collecting orchids in Panama, on 4 January he was catching butterflies and on 6 January he wrote to James Veitch of the great nursery firm of James Veitch & Son:

I went to Paraiso (Paradise) on Friday afternoon, and slept there. The scarlet passion-flower was in great beauty – but no seed. I have two slips in earth to root and bring back with me. I travelled over on a hand-car much of the way, and found another passion-flower, very pretty, and sending forth a scent such as can be equalled only by a thousand violets! '

I have sent home a box with orders that it may be sent up to you at once. You will find an Ionopsis which may be good, Pleurathalis, and some very curious Epidendra. Some seeds and a branch of the purple-and-white passion-flower, with ten seeds (unripe) and two flowers on it; also some flowers of the scarlet passion-flower: do you know this? It is brilliant: but no scent.

I came here to spend my Sunday (the Epiphany). I sail from Panama on the 10th instant, and shall be in Guatemala (D.V.) on the 18th.

But on 9 January he was dead, struck down by yellow fever. In his memorial lecture for Skinner to the Royal Horticultural Society, James Bateman declared that his friend had been responsible for introducing more new orchids into Europe than any other individual.

Most of the forty orchids described and illustrated in James Bateman's *Orchidaceae of Mexico and Guatemala*, the largest botanical book – an elephant folio – ever produced and one of the most magnificent, had been collected by Skinner. Bateman was still only twenty-six when the first part was published in 1837. It established his international reputation as a botanist and was instrumental in his election as a Fellow of the Royal Society shortly afterwards. Five further parts appeared at intervals during the following six years. All but three of the superb coloured plates were by Mrs Augusta Withers, the Flower Painter in Ordinary to Queen Adelaide (Dowager Queen after the death of

William IV in June 1837), and by Miss Drake, an accomplished botanical artist about whom little is known. The latter may well have been working on a drawing for Bateman when Jane Loddiges wrote in her diary on 8 August 1839: 'Miss Drake came to draw orchideous plants and stayed to dinner.' The plates were reproduced by lithography and coloured with great skill by hand. Bateman described each orchid in Latin and English, indicated its habitat and gave an account of its discovery and introduction to Europe. Apart from visiting the major collections of orchids in England – including those of the Duke of Devonshire, the 6th Earl of Stamford, Richard Harrison of Liverpool, the Revds John Clowes and John T. Huntley, and Loddiges' nursery – his research had taken him to Munich, Leipzig and Vienna to examine the herbaria under the care of Professor von Martius, Professor Poeppig and Dr Endlicher.

Only 125 copies of Bateman's work were printed and even if they had all been sold he would have been out of pocket by several hundreds of pounds. The list of subscribers included Queen Adelaide, to whom the work was dedicated, the King of the Belgians, the Grand Duke of Tuscany, the Dukes of Bedford, Devonshire, Marlborough, Northumberland and Sutherland, the Earls of Burlington, Derby and Powis, Earl Fitzwilliam and Earl Talbot. One copy reached the Imperial Botanic Garden in St Petersburg, where it is still the

BELOW LEFT Oncidium cavendishianum, *from James Bateman's* Orchidaceae of Mexico and Guatemala, *was named by Bateman in honour of William George Spencer Cavendish, 6th Duke of Devonshire.*

BELOW RIGHT Epidendrum stamfordianum *from the* Orchidaceae, *named by Bateman in honour of the Earl of Stamford, of Enville in Staffordshire and Dunham Massey in Cheshire.*

largest book in the Komarov Botanical Institute. The only nursery to subscribe was Loddiges', whom Bateman placed 'first on the list' among those 'who, by their zeal and skill, have brought Orchis-growing to its present palmy state'.

Some of the orchids in the book which he had introduced were named in honour of other collectors – *Oncidium cavendishianum* after the 6th Duke of Devonshire, *Cycnoches egertonianum* after Sir Philip Grey Egerton, Maria Bateman's cousin, *Epidendrum stamfordianum* after the Earl of Stamford, of Enville in Staffordshire and Dunham Massey in Cheshire, and *Stanhopea martiana* after the professor in Munich. *Cattleya skinneri* was named by Dr Lindley to commemorate both William Cattley, the first collector, and George Skinner. Bateman sent the Duke of Devonshire a prospectus of the work early in 1837 and informed him that Miss Drake was engaged in making a drawing of *Oncidium cavendishianum* which would appear in the first part. After receiving the latter the Duke wrote: 'I cannot express to you how much I am delighted by your splendid work, or how thankful I am to you for having named that most beautiful oncidium after me.'

In 1835 the Revd John Thomas Huntley of Kimbolton in Huntingdonshire, Bateman's friend and fellow-orchidist, decided to dispose of his plants, on account of financial circumstances and 'Political Apprehensions'. Bateman wrote on his behalf to the Duke of Devonshire to see if he would be interested in them, since Huntley was anxious for the collection to be kept intact rather than sold to a nursery where it would be broken up. It was Bateman's first letter to the Duke: 'It is possible that my Name may not be altogether unknown to you, as a humble Votary of the same elegant Pursuit to which your Grace has the Reputation of being warmly devoted.' Written when he was only twenty-four, it shows considerable self-confidence as well as suggesting that he had inherited some of the entrepreneurial skill of his grandfather. There were fifty specimens in Huntley's collection which Bateman knew were not represented among the Duke's plants, 'all of them too are species of the highest Rarity and Value, which till this Opportunity presented itself no Money could possibly obtain. Mr H. is anxious to dispose of his collection *entire*, and is of course aware, that a great Pecuniary Sacrifice must be incurred in so doing.' To show that he himself was disinterested Bateman continued: '. . . prior to the Offer of this Collection to yourself, Mr H. offered to give any or all of it to me, which I could never allow him to do, neither dare I venture to offer him money (although he has several Specimens that I shd esteem cheap at any Price) since I know it wd not only hurt his Feelings but immediately bring me the Plants gratis. . . N.B. Mr H. has also a few splendid & almost unique Cacti which I dare say he would be glad to dispose of with his Orchideae.' Bateman would have known that the Duke also had a cactus collection.

The Duke and Huntley exchanged letters, and Joseph Paxton was sent to inspect the orchids. Huntley was hoping for £500, and Paxton wrote to the Duke on 14 March saying that Huntley was asking a very full price for some

William George Spencer Cavendish, 6th Duke of Devonshire, President of the Horticultural Society, who shared Bateman's passion for orchids.

284 plants. 'I cannot see what sacrifice he is likely to make when he is asking as much for them as they are worth.' The Duke offered £400, but, after a meeting with Huntley at Chiswick House, raised this to £500 to be paid in three instalments over three years, which was agreed. The same John Gibson who was to bring back *Amherstia nobilis* and much else from India was sent to fetch the collection from Kimbolton.

During the course of their correspondence the Duke invited Bateman to visit Chatsworth, and Bateman extended a similar invitation to the Duke with a promise that his gardener, Patrick Don, would be 'ready (where practicable) to divide any plant that you might wish to possess'. In the event it was not the Duke but Paxton who visited Knypersley the following summer (1836), and we know from the Duke's diary that Bateman visited Chatsworth on 12 October in the same year. Before he started to collect orchids Bateman had been cultivating tropical fruits, and it was at Knypersley in 1833 that the carambola (*Averrhoa carambola*) fruited for the first time in England, on a plant he had bought from Lee's nursery in Hammersmith the previous year. Still only twenty-two, he read a paper to the Horticultural Society about this success on 3 December 1833. He also grew loquats, and the Duke had expressed an interest in seeing an example of the fruit when they met. The following February Bateman sent him a single specimen, his total crop for the year. He also sent some blimbings (the fruit of the *Averrhoa*) which, he said, were recommended for tarts or in a preserve, 'but there doubtless are in your Grace's establishment those who will refine upon these hints now thrown out'.

He told the Duke that some of his tropical fruit trees were outgrowing their accommodation at Knypersley and that he wished to send them to Chatsworth when the Great Stove was completed. 'The tree which produces the Blimbings may fairly lay claim to almost poetical beauty, with its branches profusely laden with golden fruit; and I long to see it transported to the spot where it may attain to its proper dignity.' An entry on 12 November in the Chatsworth account-book for 1837 reads: 'Paid John Gibson expenses fetching plants from Mr Batemans £5.16.4.'

Earlier that year Bateman had persuaded the Duke to support an expedition which Baron Karwinski proposed to make to Mexico. Karwinski, a Chamberlain to the King of Bavaria and an outstanding plant collector, had already spent long periods in Brazil and Mexico, where he had combined botany with mining. Dr Alexander Fisher, the Director of the Imperial Botanic Garden in St Petersburg, had the highest opinion of him – 'a better collector than he, besides poor Douglas, is not known to me'. Karwinski expressed equal confidence in his ability in a letter to Bateman: '*I dare say boldly that no other man born in Europe is more fit for such an Enterprise as I am. . . .* I have Examined with my own Eyes these botanical treasures – and I know their secret retreats, the profound and solitary ravines and vallies where they are hid, and I know how to seek for them and to find them.'

Averrhoa carambola was fruited for the first time in England by Bateman, who then read a paper on his success to the Horticultural Society at the age of twenty-two. He later presented the tree to the 6th Duke of Devonshire. The illustration is from Curtis's Botanical Magazine.

Averrhoa Carambola

ake. del.   W. Clark.

He had hoped for support from the Russian government, but Dr Fisher had been unable to obtain this for him. Bateman, who had previously received orchids collected by Karwinski, promised to support the venture in return for a share of the orchids found. At Karwinski's request he also wrote to the Duke. He offered him all the cactuses found, but explained that a third person involved was not prepared to agree to the orchids being divided between three. The Duke's reply shows that he had formed a good opinion of Bateman, for, although he had already turned down an approach from Sir William Hooker to join in this enterprise, he now responded favourably: 'I should however, from a great wish to be concerned with you in any undertaking for the increase of botanical science, and of acquisitions to our collections, be most happy to give my annual share of £100' – but only if there were 'an equal division of the harvest, as well of orchidaceae as of other things'.

In February 1838 Bateman was able to write to agree to this change in the terms he had proposed now that a Mr Wilmore of Birmingham was to be the third participant. 'This arrangement will be far more acceptable to *me*, than the one I originally proposed, as I was dying at the time for a share of the Cacteae.' He suggested that the Duke might like Paxton to be 'generalissimo in the affair', but the Duke, again showing his confidence in Bateman, replied: 'I wish at once to decline it for him – I shall greatly prefer you undertaking it, and so I am sure would he – your previous acquaintance and correspondence with Karwinski would make it desireable, in addition to the advantage we shall have in your judgement and zeal.' As a postscript to his letter he added: 'I am happy to say that the magnificent plants I received from you have got through the winter well, and are in a fine condition. The Butea superba has grown in a most surprising fashion.'

Unfortunately no further correspondence seems to have survived, but when Karwinski finally set off for Mexico in 1840 he was sponsored by the Imperial Botanic Garden in St Petersburg, and it is not clear whether Bateman and the Duke also received plants from this expedition.

On 24 April 1838 James Bateman married into one of Cheshire's most distinguished families and a family with a considerable gardening tradition. Maria Sibylla was the daughter of the Revd Rowland Egerton-Warburton of Norley Bank, near Northwich, who appears to have been an enthusiastic gardener. Other members of the family were responsible for notable gardens at Tatton Park and Oulton Park, while Maria's brother, with the help of the architect Charles Latham of Nantwich, was building an impressive new house at Arley and laying out a garden to go with it. No doubt they were related to the Peter Egerton, who, in the late seventeenth century, was described by Samuel Gilbert in the *Florist's Vade-mecum* as the best florist* in Cheshire. Maria Bateman was a very active and knowledgeable gardener with a particular interest in herbaceous plants, roses, lilies and ferns. Without her enthusiastic

*Florist in the sense of one who cultivates flowers.

Water lilies cover a large area of the lake at Biddulph Grange in August.

60

support it is unlikely that James Bateman would have embarked on such an ambitious scheme for Biddulph Grange. While orchids continued to fascinate him, his marriage led him to a much greater interest in hardy plants and garden design.

For the first few years of their marriage they lived with his parents at Knypersley Hall, which survives but in a much reduced form. Both the house and part of the garden were depicted on a Spode plate made to commemorate James Bateman's twenty-first birthday in 1832. Presumably Trubshaw's flower garden had been laid out as he designed it by 1838. The park beyond the garden appears to have been landscaped in the eighteenth century, for plantations and pools are shown on 'A Plan of the Manor and Estate of Knipersley' by James Macphail dated 1806.

We know that James Bateman landscaped part of the grounds nearer to the house, and this work may date from the years he spent at Knypersley with Maria. When Edward Cooke was taken there during his first visit to Biddulph in 1849, he was impressed by the 'most superb grounds. Noble rockwork and giant proportions'. Six years later Robert Errington, head gardener to Sir Philip Grey Egerton at Oulton Park, wrote of Knypersley in the *Cottage Gardener*: 'The mantle of Price* seems to have descended on his [Bateman's] shoulders. No tame shrubberies, insipid outlines or any kind of mannerisms may be found in his works. When he copies it is from the highest school of all – Nature.' Errington particularly admired the way Bateman had treated the large pool, around which a great variety of pleasing effects, with many inlets and promontories and some bold rock-work, had been created. The rock-work still survives. Stones from the Appian Way, Roman tablets and calcined human bones (Cooke mentions an Etruscan tomb in his diary) were placed in the recesses of the rocks. These Roman relics were perhaps collected during a visit to Italy in 1835, to which Bateman referred in a letter to the Duke of Devonshire. Errington also liked the way views of distant hills were 'borrowed' by Bateman to form part of his landscapes. Elsewhere in the garden he praised the skill of Bateman's gardener, John Sherratt, in transplanting large evergreens and the excellent state of the collection of orchids under his care.

After the birth of their second son, Rowland, in 1840 (John had been born in 1839 and Robert and Katharine were to follow), James and Maria Bateman decided to move from Knypersley Hall to Biddulph, a mile or two away, to a house which had served as the vicarage. It stood on the site of an outlying farm or grange which had once belonged to Hulton Abbey (hence Biddulph Grange). William Holt, the Vicar of Biddulph from 1831 to 1873, was James Bateman's uncle. He and his family moved from the vicarage, probably in 1841, to Elmhurst, an attractive stone house in Hurst Road. Holt placed a substantial order for plants with Caldwell's of Knutsford in that year,

*Uvedale Price (1747–1829), landscaper and author of *An Essay on the Picturesque*.

The Spode plate made to
commemorate James
Bateman's twenty-first
birthday; the views of
Knypersley Hall (centre)
and other local features were
probably drawn by
Bateman.

presumably to stock his new garden; while James Bateman placed two orders with Caldwell's in 1842, which may have been the first plants he ordered for Biddulph Grange. Unfortunately Caldwell's day books for these years, which would have listed the plants, have not survived.

When Rowland Bateman retired as Vicar of Biddulph in 1915 he presented a picture to the church which was probably painted in the 1820s and shows the church, the Church House Inn next door and the vicarage. It seems probable that Bateman retained the vicarage, altering and extending it in stages to create the Italianate mansion which was to overlook his remarkable garden.

Bateman's first recorded meeting with Edward Cooke, the man who was to play such a vital part in the creation of his garden, took place in 1847, at Kew, but they may well have met on previous occasions at Loddiges' nursery. By the time of his first visit to Biddulph, Cooke had already established a considerable reputation as a painter, particularly of marine subjects, and was a knowledgeable and enthusiastic gardener. Son of the engraver George Cooke, he was born in Chapel Street, Pentonville, in 1811 and produced drawings of great promise from an early age. When he left school he studied and worked under his father and is said also to have studied briefly under the architect Augustus Charles Pugin. The diary, which Edward Cooke kept from 1828

63

until a few days before he died on 4 January 1880, is a valuable guide to the making of the garden at Biddulph Grange and to his own development as a gardener.

George Cooke's father was born in Frankfurt-on-Main, and it may have been their common German origin which led to a close friendship with the Loddiges. Because of George Cooke's commitment to engrave the 2000 plates for George Loddiges's *Botanical Cabinet*, work which occupied him from 1817 to 1833, the Cookes moved to 4 Loddiges Place, Hackney, in 1818. While most of the drawings were by George Loddiges, a few were by Edward Cooke and by Loddiges's daughter, Jane, whom Cooke was later to marry. Edward also

OPPOSITE PAGE *The lime avenue along the western boundary of the garden predates James Bateman's layout. It leads to Biddulph church and was planted when the vicarage occupied the site of Biddulph Grange.*

LEFT *Edward Cooke admiring a fern. He was devoted to ferns, collecting them in the wild, designing fern houses and Wardian cases to grow them in and calling two of his houses The Ferns.*

helped his father with the engraving. The nursery at Hackney was the foundation of Cooke's passionate interest in plants, while he looked to George Loddiges not only for horticultural expertise but for guidance in his painting as well. 'In him had I not only a kind wellwisher and friend, but in my profession he was a most valuable adviser. His critical remarks on my pictures were so judicious that I generally adopted them without scruple or doubt.' George Loddiges was the major influence on Edward Cooke's life and career.

He was always ready with help when needed, providing transport when the Cookes moved across London from Hackney to Albion House, Barnes, in 1829, where they opened an academy for young ladies, helping in the planning of their garden and providing many of the plants. 'John Dent came with a load of plants from Mr Loddiges consisting of tall trees for Shrubbery & some American plants.' 'Mr Loddiges sent another load of Plants, Camellias, Ericas, Shrubs &c.' 'Another (fat) load of Plants from Mr Loddiges.' The Cookes had a conservatory and a vinery which produced an abundance of grapes and they made a mushroom bed in the coach-house. Their considerable collection of camellias was much admired by visitors, including the Duke of Devonshire's gardener from Chiswick House.

Later a fern house and an orchid house were added. Some of the ferns came as presents from Hackney, but Cooke collected most of them during country rambles. 'Went to Barnes Common, got ferns and planted them in my rock work.' 'I walked through the wood to Calstock and found Asp[lenium] Lanceolatum in the greatest beauty and abundance . . . filled my vasculum.' Ferns found during a long visit to Italy were kept in bottles until he returned home.

An introduction by Edwin Landseer to William Wells of Redleaf in 1836 was a significant event in Cooke's career. This shipbuilder, art collector and amateur landscape-gardener was a generous patron of young artists and invited Cooke to visit him in Kent, where he spent ten days painting, fishing and enjoying the garden and the surrounding countryside. Apart from furthering his career as a painter it was excellent preparation for the work he was to do at Biddulph. 'The flowers and plants are truly magnificent and the views most beautiful in every direction.' Wells had earned the praise of J. C. Loudon, writing in the *Gardener's Magazine* in 1839, for his skilful treatment of the landscape. Loudon was also impressed by the Dutch flower garden planted 'with a very choice selection of herbaceous plants, perhaps unequalled in the country for combining compactness and neatness of growth with beauty and rarity'. Wells had designed everything himself, producing working drawings for the landscaping, gardens and buildings, including a rustic orangery and a rustic billiard-room in the Dutch garden. Two gardeners' cottages were constructed from materials found on the estate under his personal supervision.

But it is the use of rocks at Redleaf which makes it notable in the history of English gardens. Wells very effectively exposed a considerable area of rock

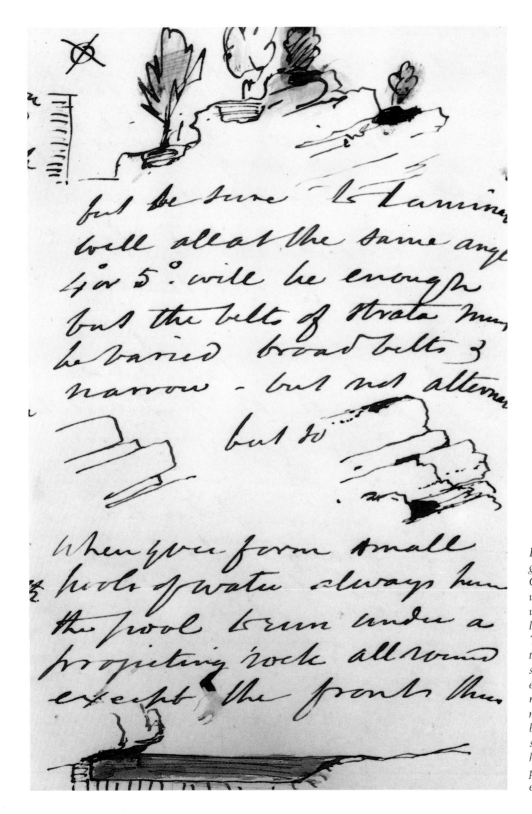

In his later work as a garden designer, Edward Cooke was very specific with his advice on rock-work, as this page from a letter to a Mr Roper shows. The text reads: 'but be sure to laminate well all at the same angle, 4° or 5° will be enough but the belts of strata may be varied broad belts & narrow – but not alternate – but so. . . . When you form small pools of water always have the pool to run under a projecting rock all round except the fronts, thus.'

which lay just under the surface of the ground and simulated further outcrops on the large lawn, producing more realistic effects than had been achieved before. These features influenced Cooke's later work as a designer of gardens and stimulated his interest in rocks as a painter, an interest probably first kindled by his father, who had engraved plates of geological features in coastal scenery and for John Pinkerton's *Petrology, or a Treatise on the Rocks* (1811). When Edward Cooke was later elected to a Fellowship of the Royal Society his Certificate of Candidature described him as eminent as a 'Landscape and Marine Painter – and as a faithful delineator of Geological features in nature'. His appreciation of the picturesque quality of old stumps, which were to be used so effectively at Biddulph, may also have been aroused at Redleaf, where 'Mr Wells selected stumps and old pieces of wood which I painted into a picture'. Wells paid the young artist most generously for his work.

Another important influence on Cooke was Nathaniel Ward, whom he had probably met through George Loddiges and who became a close friend. Cooke frequently visited Ward at Wellclose Square and later at Clapham Rise, admiring the splendid collection of plants and adding further to his botanical education. They enjoyed each other's company and rambled and botanised together in Kent, Devon, the Lake District and Scotland. An acquaintance wrote of them: 'There was much in common in the two men, the same lovable character, the same appreciation of what was pure and good and beautiful – the same keen love of Nature in all her manifestations, the same sympathy with knowledge and progress, the same freedom from petty affectations and shams, the same generosity towards others.' (*Gardeners' Chronicle*, 1880). The bond was further strengthened in April 1848, when Cooke's sister, Georgiana, married Ward's son Stephen.

Cooke fell under the spell of orchids in 1842. Work was in progress on his orchid house – 'kiddy-house' – in May, and there were frequent gifts of orchids from Hackney – 'all day with Mr George selecting Palms & Kiddies & ferns for my house'. 'Mr Loddiges gave me a box of 14 orchideous plants.' 'Con selected about 50 orchids and we packed them up.' He had a second orchid house by the end of September and spent a great deal of time making different containers for his plants. Some were placed in half coconuts, as they were at Loddiges'. Others were fixed to artificial trees made of lichen-covered branches and twigs gathered in the country. In October Cooke recorded that he had been to Hackney to study Loddiges' copy of Bateman's book on the orchids of Guatemala and Mexico. He was later to be given a copy.

Cooke continued to live at Barnes until 1849. The later years there had brought much sadness through the deaths of three of his sisters, his father, his grandfather, his baby daughter and, in 1843, his wife Jane, less than three years after their marriage, who left behind two small sons. Then, when he was in Italy in 1846, he received the news of the death of George Loddiges, which he described in his diary as 'the most bitterly distressing news I have ever had'. 'I can find none to take his place', he wrote to a friend.

In 1849 he moved with his mother and unmarried sisters to a house in Victoria Road, Kensington, which he called The Ferns, and where he again devoted a good deal of time to planning the garden, making a model of it in clay. Here, too, some elements in the garden – the fernery and the use of a stumpery as a picturesque setting for plants – anticipated similar features at Biddulph. A grotto was constructed in the hothouse using a wagon-load of stone from Redleaf, an 'aquarium' was arranged in the rockery and bananas were planted in the greenhouse. Many plants were brought from the Barnes garden, including 'a 2 horse load of camellias', but Cooke owed many others to the kindness of his friends. A load of trees arrived from Hackney; a considerable number of plants were received from Cox, the gardener at Redleaf; James Bateman sent a fine collection of stove plants and ferns; and Dr Lindley provided seven vines of different sorts. A large crate of ivies, conifers and rock plants was dispatched from his nursery in Canterbury by William Masters, who visited the garden shortly afterwards with his wife and son. A few plants were bought from E. G. Henderson & Sons, of Pineapple Place, Edgware Road, London, while foxgloves, anemones, orchises and ferns were brought back from rambles in the country.

Cooke now felt ready to offer his services as a garden designer. He had seen many fine gardens when staying at the country houses of his rich patrons and had visited famous gardens during his travels in France, Holland and Italy. He had also acquired a considerable knowledge of plants, had developed two gardens of his own and had many ideas about the making of gardens. His first venture was to help Nathaniel Ward when he moved to Clapham Rise, noting in his diary on 17 January 1848 that he 'wrote to Mr Ward with *suggestions for his new garden*!!!'. A month afterwards he designed Ward's new fernery and met the builder on the site to discuss details.

He was also designing Wardian cases – he had been using 'Warderies' for a number of years – and was responsible for some of those he and Ward showed to the public at the Great Exhibition of 1851. On the eve of the opening he wrote in his diary: 'Went to the Exhibn. at 8, very busy all day . . . Mr Ward came and left at 5. I got the tables made and one covered with cloth and 8 cases were put up. Prince Albert, the Queen and a large party came. At 3 a rehearsal of God Save the Queen and Hallelujah Chorus – 700 performers – glorious music.' He was on duty on 2 June and ready to meet the Queen: 'Went at half p 8 to the Exhibition, to receive the Queen and explain the Fern cases, but she did not visit my stand.'

Two years earlier he had received his first invitation to visit the Batemans. On the morning of Friday 7 September 1849 he took a cab to Euston for the ten o'clock express train and reached Congleton in Cheshire at half past four. Mr Bateman's gig was waiting at the station, and by five o'clock he was at Biddulph Grange.

FOUR

Bringing the World to Biddulph

Edward Cooke's first visit to Biddulph lasted seven days, and he was impressed by what he saw both at Biddulph Grange and at Knypersley Hall. He was equally impressed by the surrounding countryside at Knypersley when John Bateman took him for 'a delightful stroll to the Gorton stone and Well, the Hermitage, and into the little castellated building [the warder's tower] – home by the Great Lakes and the Burn, most lovely scenery and rocks'.

Much of this first visit was spent designing 'various things in the gardens' and making improvements to the fernery through which the main entrance to the house was then approached. Cooke designed rock-work for the fernery and elsewhere with the aid of clay models. He also made designs for a pinfold (cattle pound) in Knypersley and for a church – Christ Church – and a parsonage in the village of Biddulph Moor. The pinfold was erected at Red Cross opposite the school. In 1911 it had to make way for an additional school building, but the stone entrance wall, with the carved head of a bull, was retained as part of the school wall and may still be seen.

As with Cooke's later visits to Biddulph, work on the gardens was combined with a range of social activities which reflected the interests he shared with Bateman. They visited the Minton Hollins tile factory in Stoke and lunched with Herbert Minton, who was also an orchid enthusiast and a subscriber to the *Orchidaceae*. Minton Hollins tiles were used in the house and the garden at Biddulph Grange. From Stoke they drove to Trentham, where the Revd E. J. Edwards (another subscriber) guided them round the celebrated gardens of the 2nd Duke of Sutherland and then took them back to the vicarage for tea and to see his ferns. Before returning to Biddulph they heard a lecture by Professor Owen in Stoke town hall on the extinct birds of New Zealand and then called to see the School of Design.

During the following seventeen years Cooke paid a further fifteen visits to Biddulph and frequently exchanged letters with James and occasionally with Maria. He and Bateman also met from time to time in London to discuss plans, either at Cooke's home or at the Athenaeum, where they were members. They clearly enjoyed each other's company, for in London, as at Biddulph, the study of garden plans was combined with social engagements – visits to the Lord Mayor's Show, the Great Exhibition, the British Museum and the Surrey Gardens, famed for fireworks and panoramic displays. They attended a recital from *Nicholas Nickleby* and *The Pickwick Papers* by Charles Dickens, and arranged an excursion to Brunel's latest ship, the *Great Eastern*, accompanied by the sculptor Waterhouse Hawkins.

Edward Cooke probably designed all the architectural features in the garden at Biddulph. He frequently made models of what he designed and he also played an active part in building rock-work, planting trees and shrubs, and gathering ferns and other native plants in the wild for the garden.

James and Maria Bateman shared Cooke's enthusiasm for ferns, and the fern garden, which the latter admired and helped to perfect during his first visit, provided a striking approach to the house. In his first series of articles about Biddulph Grange which appeared in the *Gardeners' Chronicle* in 1856 the landscape gardener Edward Kemp described it as a 'little rocky dell' with a small stream flowing through it by a path which led to the door of the house. On one side there were illuminated recesses, each housing a rare fern, and on the other a fern garden with moss-covered rock-work to a height of 10 or 12

The south front of the house James Bateman designed, from the 1871 sale catalogue.

feet associated with hollies, mahonias and other shrubs. 'Coming so suddenly and unexpectedly on this delightful little scene, which, with its green luxuriance of vegetation and its delicious shade and repose, offers the most pleasing welcome after the fatigues and discomforts of a journey – especially in warm or dusty weather – the mind is well prepared for receiving subsequent agreeable impressions; and not even the perfume of the richest and gayest flowers, however tastefully clustered about the entrance, vestibule or corridor, appear calculated to convey so agreeable a greeting as this little choice bit of wild nature, with its cool freshness and greenness.' Most of the British ferns were represented – many of them had been found within a few miles of Biddulph – as well as some hardy exotic species. The windows of the dining-room looked out into this fern garden. When a second dining-room was built, the fernery was replaced by an open court.

Bateman himself was the architect of the house, which, with some help from Cooke and a draughtsman, he developed and extended over a period of more than twenty years. The Italianate mansion he created may well have been influenced by Osborne House on the Isle of Wight, designed by Prince Albert with the assistance of the builder Thomas Cubitt. Unfortunately most of Bateman's house was burnt down in 1896 (see p. 151), but early photographs show that it was an impressive achievement, though certain rather awkward and amateurish features before it was further altered, such as the tunnel which continued the line of the south-front terrace through a projecting wing to the east and the windowless service rooms and butler's quarters immediately behind it, may be seen as confirmation that Bateman was altering and extending the existing vicarage rather than building an entirely new house.

Bateman paid as much attention to the detail of the interiors as he did to the garden and spent lavishly on the main rooms. The dining-room had a parquetry floor, an inlaid wood ceiling, spiral fluted red pine columns and gilt Italian leather panels. The marble mantelpiece had been bought in 1822 at the sale of the contents of Fonthill, William Beckford's extraordinary gothic pile in Wiltshire, and probably first installed at Knypersley Hall and moved to the Grange after John Bateman's death. It was 11 feet long with carved panels of Orpheus taming the wild beasts, Apollo and the Muses, and the founding of Troy. The dining-room looked into a colonnaded 'classical court or *hypethra*', paved with ornamental tiles. Hellebores, periwinkles and climbers grew in a border, while a central bed of skimmia, retinospora (cypresses) and golden and variegated thuja was set within a Grecian pattern of red and white sand. This open court was derived from the peristyle of Greek and Roman houses.

It was one of many classical echoes at Biddulph. The library, which would have housed a fine collection of botanical and gardening books, was inspired by ancient Greece, with a white and gold panelled ceiling and two marble mantelpieces. The classical billiard-room had a glass ceiling supported on Corinthian columns and was separated by glass from a fern house (initially the

rhododendron house) of similar style. There was an 'exquisitely designed mantel piece with Caryatides and friezes' in the oak room or drawing-room. (This room was also embellished with eleven carved groups of flowers and fruit set between spiral pillars on the walls.)

From a small picture gallery a flight of steps led down to 'a model of two chambers of a Roman catacomb or tomb, with early pagan inscriptions on the walls'. There were Roman features in the garden, too – four paving-stones from the Appian Way placed round an ash tree in the arboretum, antique Roman heads in a wall near the entrance to the house and a Roman tripod on the eastern terrace, which was approached through a stone archway surmounted by an eagle.

On the first floor of the house there were, according to the sale catalogue, fourteen principal bedrooms, as well as a boudoir, a studio, an orangery and a conservatory-corridor, with sixteen other rooms 'for bachelors and servants' on the second floor. And there were ten water-closets. The lighting was by gas and the heating by hot water passing through 'an immense length of iron piping'. Three carriage houses could accommodate nine carriages.

The Batemans lost no opportunity to bring the garden into the house. Apart from the fern house, the orangery, the conservatory-corridor and the open court, there was also a camellia house between the drawing-room and the

The billiard room in 1871 with the fern house beyond, originally built to house the rhododendrons from the glen.

73

library. The conservatory-corridor, which was devoted to tender fruits, led from the rooms of James and Maria Bateman to the upper terrace at the east end of the house, enabling them to reach the garden without first going down to the ground floor.

Flowers were extensively used to decorate the house. Orchids would have been prominent among them and were particularly recommended by Bateman as table decorations. Even when he was staying in London the hothouses at Knypersley kept him supplied with flowers. On 2 June 1837 he wrote from Maynard's Hotel in Albemarle Street to Sir William Hooker: 'While in Town all the Orchidaceae (as they come into bloom) are cut and sent up hither to furnish my rooms.' When the Bishop of Lichfield was expected to luncheon at Biddulph Grange, Edward Cooke was at work before breakfast arranging evergreens in the dining-room. The original paintings by Miss Drake and Mrs Withers for the book on Mexican and Guatemalan orchids lined the walls of the corridor which led from the entrance hall to the drawing-room, where there were probably Wardian cases with ferns and other plants.

The attention paid to the integration of house and garden was also evident in the area of the garden nearest the house, which was planned to harmonise with the building. Kemp was impressed by the way this was achieved: 'All the

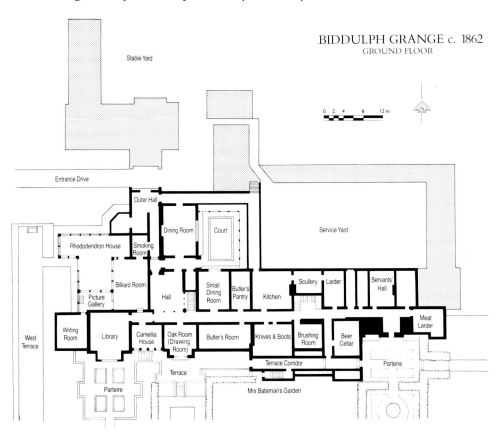

BIDDULPH GRANGE c. 1862
GROUND FLOOR

A conjectural plan of Biddulph Grange in 1862, which shows how the rhododendron house (later the fern house), the camellia house, the dining-room court, the conservatory corridor and the orangery brought the garden into the house.

ground in front of the principal windows, and that which comes into direct association with the house, has an artistic character peculiar to itself. Terrace platforms, ornamental walls, corridors, and arches in complete agreement with the style of the house, trim hedges, elaborate parterres, stone edgings to the walks, or plants that blend well with architectural objects, have all been most carefully introduced.'

The Batemans laid out a series of formal gardens, framed by imposing and immaculate yew hedges, between the south front of the house and the lake, terracing the slope to create three different levels. Much of this had probably been established before they sought the help of Edward Cooke. Kemp's plan (see p. 8), published with his second series of articles in the *Gardeners' Chronicle* in 1862, shows the extent of these gardens at that date.

Below the library at the west end of the house a small parterre was divided into four beds, which were filled with bedding plants in summer. East of this, in front of the drawing-room, a flight of steps led down to the mosaic parterre, where hybrid China roses were planted in four beds round a box-edged mosaic pattern of red and white sand. A second flight led to a fountain, not installed until after Kemp's visit, and a third to the araucaria parterre, enclosed by a stone balustrade, with four monkey puzzles in a framework of clipped yew. At the

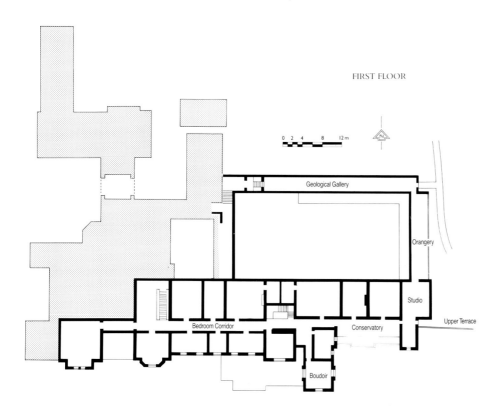

FIRST FLOOR

0 2 4 8 12 m

Geological Gallery

Orangery

Studio

Upper Terrace

Bedroom Corridor

Conservatory

Boudoir

east end of the house, beyond the terrace tunnel, the verbena parterre was planted with verbenas and other bedding plants. Below it, through an arch of roses, lay the rose parterre and beyond that the dahlia walk.

. Maria Bateman's private garden occupied the space between the rose parterre and the mosaic parterre and was approached through a concealed door in the tunnel. It was completely secluded on three sides by tall yew hedges and on the fourth by the wall of the house – a secret garden, in fact. Her boudoir was above the tunnel and looked down into this garden, which was said by Kemp to afford 'every facility for lady gardening', whatever that may have meant. It was devoted to bulbs, herbaceous plants and 'any other rare things which individual fancy may select'.

Unfortunately there is no detailed contemporary description of this garden, but it must have been one of the most interesting areas at Biddulph, for Maria Bateman was a connoisseur of herbaceous plants at a time when they were not generally appreciated. Most gardens were being laid out with formal beds of tender plants, raised under glass by the thousand, their red, pink, yellow, blue and white flowers used like paint. Traditional hardy garden plants, previously admired for the beauty of their form, were rejected in favour of plants which were low-growing and could be regimented into bold masses of colour – pelargoniums, calceolarias, lobelias, verbenas, petunias, alyssums, salvias, heliotropes. 'Everyone now, down to the farmers' wives', wrote Henry Kingsley in *Argosy*, 'are discontented unless they have their beds brown and bare for six months, and for the other six filled with formal patterns of geraniums, calceolarias, and lobelias'. The Batemans were exceptions to this rule, and Kemp was delighted to find at Biddulph 'all the beautiful

ABOVE *The line of the terrace fronting Biddulph Grange continued through the terrace tunnel and up a flight of steps to the Wellingtonia avenue and the obelisk walk. The framework of clipped yew dividing the formal gardens can be seen on the right. The photograph was taken in 1905.*

OPPOSITE PAGE *The view of the Italian garden, as it came to be called, seen from the library in 1871. The framework has changed little, and most of the planting has been renewed.*

OPPOSITE PAGE Dahlia
imperialis *from* Curtis's
Botanical Magazine. *In the
dahlia walk Bateman planted
some of the beds with single
colours and some with mixed
colours.*

BELOW *The dahlia walk
and the garden house,
photographed in 1905, ceased
to exist when Biddulph
Grange became a hospital in
1924, but are now being
restored by the National
Trust.*

Delphiniums, Phloxes, Penstemons, and many other tribes, which the modern system of flower gardening has almost banished from our gardens'.

While Maria probably preferred softer shades and subtler combinations in her borders, James liked to group strong colours and bold forms. Dahlias, with their exotic shapes and bright colours, were his kind of flower. They had become very fashionable in England during the first half of the nineteenth century, and British nurserymen and gardeners were said 'to illuminate the northern part of the globe by the full brilliancy of these floral luminaries, which now shine as conspicuously in our groves as gas in our towns' (Henry Phillips, *Flora Historica*). Considerable space was allotted to them at Biddulph, where the long, stepped dahlia walk extended from the fountain below the mosaic parterre to the garden house below the eastern terrace. Again there was a firm framework of yew, with a tall backing hedge from which buttresses of yew projected to form compartments that corresponded with the stretches of level ground between the steps in the path. The buttresses of yew which divide the

remarkable herbaceous borders at Arley Hall may have been inspired by those at Biddulph. Bateman planted some of the compartments with single colours, others with mixed colours. Like Mrs Bateman's garden, the dahlia walk could not be seen easily from other parts of the garden and could be avoided when the flowers were past their best.

To the east, the line of the main, south-facing terrace continued through the cherry orchard (which later became a rose garden) and the arboretum to the Wellingtonia avenue and eventually to the moor beyond. In the cherry orchard cherries and other fruit trees were planted in rows on mounds, all pruned to uniform shape with cotoneasters clipped to resemble a bell round each tree. A range of clematis supported by chains bordered the path. One of the clematis grown at Biddulph was the deep purple Jackmannii, which Bateman praised in a lecture to the Royal Horticultural Society in 1865, recommending that it should be planted in association with the azure blue clematis, *C. lanuginosa*. No doubt these two plants were joined at Biddulph by the clematis which the nurseryman George Jackman named 'Mrs James Bateman' in 1867.

The arboretum was of limited size and range. There were a number of maples and liquidambars, selected for their striking colours, as well as oaks, hollies, various thorns, gorse, gaultherias, spiraeas, japonicas and heaths. A small pool was surrounded with pampas grass (*Cortaderia selloana*), *Osmunda regalis* ferns and a mass of the white-stemmed bramble *Rubus biflorus*.

To plant the Wellingtonia avenue Bateman obtained some of the earliest specimens of this tree to reach Britain. An editorial in the *Gardeners' Chronicle* on 24 December 1853 announced that Veitch & Son had received branches and cones of a remarkable tree from their collector in California, William Lobb. Lobb had described it as 'the monarch of the Californian forest', because of its great size. One specimen which had been felled was more than 300 feet in length and was reckoned to be 3000 years old – 'it must have been a little plant when Samson was slaying the Philistines'. The writer of the editorial had no doubts about what the tree should be named: 'We think that no one will differ from us in feeling that the most appropriate name to be proposed for the most gigantic tree which has been revealed to us is that of the greatest of modern heroes. WELLINGTON stands as high above his contemporaries as the Californian tree above all the surrounding foresters. Let it then bear henceforth the name of WELLINGTONIA GIGANTEA. Emperors and Kings and princes have their plants, and we must not forget to place in the highest rank among them our own great warrior.' Six months later in the same publication Veitch & Son offered seedling Wellingtonias for sale at £2.2.0 each, reducing to £1.1.0 each if twelve plants were bought. Bateman almost certainly bought some of these.

Bateman planted his Wellingtonias alternately with deodars, as part of a complex planting scheme which was probably influenced by the avenues at the 4th Earl of Harrington's Elvaston Castle near Derby. Terrace banks planted

with red horse chestnuts (*Aesculus x carnea*) backed by Austrian pines (*Pinus nigra*) provided shelter on either side, with white-flowered briar roses (*Rosa arvensis*) covering the slopes of the banks. It was Bateman's intention eventually to remove the deodars, but, for some reason, his successor Robert Heath chose to remove the Wellingtonias instead. It is hoped that the National Trust will eventually restore them.

At the end of the Wellingtonia avenue a high yew hedge surrounds the enormous stone vase, which, until the death of John Bateman, stood in the grounds of Knypersley Hall. The straight walk which continues beyond it is now overgrown, but the bordering woodland and heather was once carefully managed and the path kept well sanded. This steeply rising path created the remarkable optical illusion of a stone obelisk against a dark background and was known as the obelisk walk. Staffordshire Moorlands District Council has undertaken to restore it. At the end of the path a tunnel led through the rock to a gamekeeper's cottage, dog kennels and pheasant nursery, enabling the gamekeeper to pass in and out of the wood without being observed by poachers. A return walk through the woods to the north of the Wellingtonia avenue rejoined the eastern terrace.

A tall beech hedge along the eastern terrace concealed the Egyptian court from the rest of the garden. A screen of yews across the gap in the hedge where the path led to the pyramid completed the concealment and ensured the element of surprise. Visitors turning into the court were suddenly confronted by the stone sphinxes, yew obelisks and pyramid. The obelisks were fashioned

Sequoiadendron giganteum, the Wellingtonia (left). The Wellingtonia avenue was planted with some of the earliest specimens to reach Britain and interplanted, as a temporary measure, with deodar cedars (right), but Bateman's successor, Robert Heath, removed the Wellingtonias. Both illustrations are from Pinetum Britannicum.

An aquatint of the Egyptian court by Norman Stevens, who simplified the composition by omitting one pair of sphinxes.

82

very skilfully with golden yew trained to form a well-defined band between the dark yew of the plinth and the column. The upper part of the pyramid was most ingeniously created from yews planted in narrow brick troughs above the Cheshire cottage.

The monstrous statue inside the pyramid represents the Ape of Thoth, an associate of the god Thoth whom the Egyptians credited with inventing botany. The ape and the sphinxes were probably the work of Waterhouse Hawkins, as were the ox and the frog in 'China'. Cooke may have provided the model for the ape, since he recorded buying at auction on 14 September 1861 at J. C. Stevens's sale rooms 'small skeletons, Mexican Idols and Egyptian Gods'.

Some features at Biddulph were probably suggested by similar features in French *jardins anglo-chinois*, so called because they were regarded as having their roots in China as well as in England. The idea of placing the Egyptian pyramid back-to-back with the Cheshire cottage may well have been inspired by the cottage in the garden of the Comte d'Harcourt at Chaillot in France, which became a Turkish tent when you passed through the front door. This was illustrated by the author George-Louis Le Rouge in his *Détails des nouveaux jardins à la mode* (1776–88), which may have been in Bateman's library. The

BELOW LEFT *The monstrous stone figure inside the Egyptian pyramid represents the Ape of Thoth, an associate of the god Thoth whom the Egyptians credited with the invention of botany.*

BELOW RIGHT *The rear entrance of the Egyptian pyramid turns out to be a Cheshire cottage, one of the garden's many surprises.*

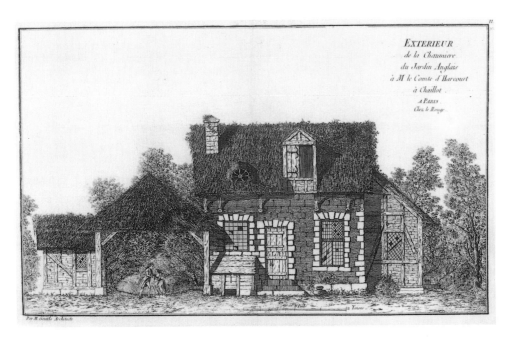

Egyptian style became popular in French gardens as a result of Napoleon's campaigns in Egypt, and there are plans of Egyptian temples in J. C. Krafft's *Plans des plus beaux jardins pittoresques* (1809–10), which Bateman and Cooke may have studied. One of them is accompanied by sphinxes and has the same common winged device over the entrance which appears at Biddulph; an illustration in another volume by the same author shows an Egyptian temple associated with two obelisks, though of stone not yew.

Bateman probably got his idea for a Cheshire cottage leading into an Egyptian pyramid from illustrations in Le Rouge's Détails des nouveaux jardins à la mode, *which show a cottage which led into a Turkish tent in a garden in Chaillot.*

Cooke made many plans for the Cheshire cottage which forms a surprise exit from Egypt. Appropriately, the building has a cornice of cones of *Pinus pinea* cut in half, for this and two large stone cones of *Pinus coulteri* placed outside the cottage introduce the pinetum. A pinetum, in the strictest sense, is a collection of pines, but it is generally understood to mean a collection of conifers. (Edward Cooke also used the word 'conetum', which he may have coined himself.) The idea of assembling such collections, as distinct from general collections of trees, was a response to the wealth of exciting new species introduced by David Douglas and other collectors in the early and mid nineteenth century. The Douglas fir, the deodar, the Atlas cedar, the Japanese cedar and the Wellingtonia were all introduced between 1826 and 1853, while the monkey puzzle, though discovered somewhat earlier, became freely available then for the first time.

Some pinetums were merely collections of single trees planted on a flat piece of ground without any element of design, but Bateman was more interested in creating an aesthetically pleasing garden than in compiling a scientific catalogue. At the same time he paid great attention to the individual requirements of different species, placing them in relatively exposed or sheltered situations as they required, and providing dry sandy conditions for some and moist heavier soils for others.

Many tons of earth had to be moved to produce the gently rising slopes on either side of the path, while mounds of varying shapes and height were formed on which to plant many of the trees so that they would not be exposed to too much moisture at the base and in order to display them more effectively. In using mounds in this way Bateman was influenced by J. C. Loudon's Derby Arboretum, Britain's first public park, laid out in 1840. Various plants were used as ground cover on the mounds, in some cases common heather, *Calluna vulgaris*, in others various heaths – *Erica carnea*, *Erica ciliaris* and *Erica multiflora* – or bilberries mingled with ferns.

In front of the Cheshire cottage there was a fine 'Densa' juniper – *Juniperus recurva* 'Densa' – on either side of the path, which Edward Kemp described as 'green fountains'. They were backed by other junipers, including species from China introduced by Robert Fortune, and cypresses. Beyond them there were impressive groups of monkey puzzles and deodars to the left of the path and deodars and pines to the right, with a view of the church the Batemans had built at Knypersley straight ahead until the trees eventually obscured it. Bateman preferred to use groups of trees rather than single trees, but each tree in the group was given plenty of room to develop, while the spacing of the trees was irregular.

Colour effects in the pinetum were carefully planned. Heathers covered the mounds on which many of the trees were planted; groups of golden hollies and golden yews served as foils to monkey puzzles and deodars; dark yews and hollies were used as background for lighter greens; a large group of gorse

Apart from the deodars in the Wellingtonia avenue, Bateman also planted some specimens on mounds in the pinetum so that they could be seen to better advantage.

86

There are some very large monkey puzzles, Araucaria araucana, *in the pinetum at Biddulph, and James Bateman also used them in a formal parterre. The illustration is from* Pinetum Britannicum.

OPPOSITE PAGE *Many plants survive from the nineteenth century in the rhododendron ground, but it is not always easy to determine which were planted by Bateman and which by Heath.*

provided further relief; and scarlet oaks were particularly valuable in autumn. Other varieties of oak and a number of thorns were also planted among the conifers.

At the far end of the pinetum, as one approached the tunnel through the rock leading to the rhododendron ground, there were groups of pines and firs. 'Next to the Orchidaceae my delight is in the Pines', Bateman wrote to Sir William Hooker, '& I am dying for a copy of the Duke of Bedford's work on his Pinetum at Woburn.' Several other less hardy pine species were planted round the irregularly shaped and very unusual bowling green, which was

Rhododendron falconeri, *introduced from Sikkim by Joseph Hooker in 1850 and planted in the glen by Bateman, who described it as 'nearly but not quite hardy'.*

formed between the pinetum and 'China'. Among them were *Pinus ponderosa* and *Pinus radiata*, both introduced by Douglas.

Bateman was also devoted to rhododendrons and azaleas and cultivated a considerable collection in the rhododendron ground, which they shared with other 'American plants', as shrubs requiring acid soils were known regardless of country of origin. Here they included large masses of *Kalmia augustifolia*, *Pieris floribunda* and *Gaultheria shallon* (another Douglas introduction).

Striking use of rhododendrons and azaleas was made by the lime avenue below the western terrace where Bateman planted a semi-circular tiered bank with varieties of strong colour which would flower at the same time – the Rainbow. Perhaps this was an echo of the Rainbow Walk at Trentham, where

two beds on either side of a long gravel path were planted in the colours of the rainbow.

The stars of the rhododendron collection should have been the species from Sikkim and Bhutan which had been introduced by Joseph Hooker and others. Bateman went to great lengths to construct an appropriate habitat for them after carefully studying Hooker's *Himalayan Journals*. 'I fitted up for their reception a dark rocky glen through which there ran a stream of water, thus ensuring shade and constant moisture.' The best quality peat was provided, and the rhododendrons – among them *Rhododendron thomsonii, R. fulgens, R. falconeri, R. hodgsonii* and *R. ciliatum* – were planted against perpendicular masses of rock facing north and sheltered from the wind. This situation was

Rhododendron ciliatum, another of Joseph Hooker's introductions (1850) from Sikkim, was planted by Bateman in the glen.

The stream from 'China' runs through a rocky channel in the glen, which was constructed to Edward Cooke's design.

chosen to retard growth and thus to reduce frost damage. All seems to have gone well for a year or two, but when the plants failed to flower Bateman decided to move them into an Ormson conservatory erected by the west side of the house. They seemed to be settling down quite well, but then Bateman read an article in the *Gardeners' Chronicle* which described the climate of Sikkim as very hot and humid during the growing season. He decided that he must try to reproduce similar conditions in his rhododendron house with very disappointing results, since none of the plants benefited from the change and some of them suffered greatly. He continued to grow rhododendrons under glass, but what had formerly been called the rhododendron house was called the fern house in the catalogue prepared for the sale of the estate in 1871.

The transfer of the rhododendrons from the glen coincided with the removal of the fern garden by the entrance to the house, and the very considerable collection of British and foreign ferns was replanted in the glen. The glen also supported a wide range of semi-aquatic plants, marsh plants, bog plants, exotic grasses, butterworts, cranberries and bamboos. For these, too, Bateman tried to provide the ideal conditions. 'In truth, here, as everywhere throughout the place, the greatest possible peculiarity of condition is introduced, not merely for the sake of additional variety (though that has been one element of consideration) but to furnish a congenial abode for that wondrous multitude of curious or ornamental plants to which such circumstances are naturally incident' (Kemp).

The scale and quality of the rock-work in the glen is remarkable, and it is also used extensively and effectively elsewhere in the rhododendron ground and in 'China'. In earlier gardens rock was used principally in the construction of grottoes. Eighteenth-century English landscapers did not make much use of rock-work, although existing rocks were exploited in a number of gardens, most notably at Hawkstone in Shropshire, Piercefield in the Wye Valley and Studley Royal in North Yorkshire. On the Continent, however, there was more interest in rocks. At Sanspareil near Bayreuth, a spectacularly rocky site was transformed into a most impressive early landscape garden for the Margravine Wilhelmine. In France Le Rouge published an engraving of natural rocks as a guide for the makers of gardens, while Hubert Robert, painter and garden designer, made outstandingly effective use of rock-work at Versailles and the Petit Trianon.

Repton advocated the naturalistic use of rock-work, which had to be done so judiciously 'that the interference of art shall never be detected'. At Thoresby, in Nottinghamshire, he set about transforming the cascade by divesting it of its 'disgusting and artificial formality' and transporting from Cresswell Crags 'the rocky bed of a mountain stream, and some larger masses of stone together with the bushes that were growing in their fissures'. He also used rock-work at Sezincote in Gloucestershire and Welbeck Abbey in Nottinghamshire. An early nineteenth-century garden noted for its rocks was Lady Broughton's

The entrance of the tunnel which leads from the rhododendron ground to the pinetum, another feature designed by Edward Cooke.

Hoole House, near Chester, but there nature was not imitated in the way Repton intended but by constructing a large-scale model of the mountains of Savoy. Redleaf in Kent was, as we have seen, remarkable for the way William Wells exploited the abundance of rock just below the surface, while rock-work on a large scale ('tens of thousands of tons') was used at Elvaston Castle by William Barron, one of the nineteenth century's most famous head gardeners, and at Chatsworth by Joseph Paxton. Both gardens were known to Bateman.

The use of rocks at Biddulph may well have been influenced by 'An Essay on Rockwork in Garden Scenery', which appeared in the *Gardener's Magazine* in 1831. The author advised that it was essential 'to observe the manner in which masses of rocks are disposed in nature, or rather in such natural scenes as are admired by men of taste, and especially painters. And here the study of geology will materially assist both the painter and gardener.' The gardener should base any rock-work he intended to construct on some natural rock-work known to him, 'but if he does not feel confidence in himself, we would recommend him to take the advice of a landscape-painter who has been accustomed to rocky countries'.

While Bateman had already used rocks himself at Knypersley, he could hardly have chosen anyone better qualified than Edward Cooke to design the rock-work at Biddulph. The pillars of stone in the Chinese water are a good example of his skill in rock-landscaping, while the very extensive use of rock in the glen was praised by Kemp for its naturalness. 'The numberless stones are all piled together on their natural bed, and there is nothing whatever to be seen of the usual rock-builder's trick of standing stones on their edges or their ends for the sake of giving prominence to any point, or producing a greater ruggedness of surface.'

Both Bateman and Cooke would have found inspiration in the remarkable outcrops of red sandstone on Biddulph Moor. All the stone used in the garden is almost certainly Chatsworth gritstone from Troughstone Hill, a mile or two north-east of Biddulph Grange and presumably so named because it was a source of stone for drinking troughs. The straight, stone-surfaced track of even gradient, down which it was brought from the quarry in trucks, still survives in part, though the rails are no longer there. It was not far from Troughstone Hill to the Grange, but the labour involved would have been considerable.

Root-work was an alternative to rock-work in Victorian gardens. 'In localities where stone is not easily procured,' wrote Edward Kemp in *How to Lay Out a Garden*, 'or where it abounds so much that some other material would be preferable, the *rugged stumps* or *roots* of old trees may be substituted, and will yield quite as much picturesqueness.' Bateman made a notable stumpery by the approach to 'China' from the eastern terrace. Tree stumps were piled up and secured to a height of 10 or 12 feet on either side of the winding path, meeting overhead in places. 'Mr Bateman has been singularly fortunate in procuring a quantity of the most gnarled, contorted, and varied

A simulated outcrop in the rhododendron ground, almost certainly using stone from the quarry on Troughstone Hill.

masses of wood imaginable for this purpose; and they are joined together and disposed with exquisite art' (Kemp). This framework provided Bateman with a range of conditions in which to grow a variety of plants. 'Over considerable portions of the whole, masses of Ivy, Virginian Creeper, Cotoneaster, and other trailing plants scramble about in the wildest manner. And the interstices, as well as the open spaces now and then occurring at the base, are all used for the reception of some characteristic and interesting plant or group. For example, near the entrance to this region, the Hellebores, which are among the earliest of the winter-flowering plants, are clustered in great variety. Then follow the Anemones, Epimediums, Scillas, Uvularias, Lilies of the Valley, etc., each kind receiving the precise amount of sunlight or shade which is desirable for it, and all being mingled with Gaultherias, Pernettyas, Cotoneasters, Savins, and such dwarf evergreens as serve to produce a sufficiency of green clothing at all seasons of the year.'

Root-work also featured on a steep bank in the rhododendron ground where a ground cover of Irish ivy (*Hedera helix* 'Hibernica') and parsley-leaved bramble (*Rubus laciniatus*) trailed over old roots and stumps for picturesque effect. Here Kemp was impressed by the way Bateman, 'with a judicious disregard for petty criticism', had planted dead trees upside-down in the ground, with their roots 8 or 10 feet in the air, and had trained ivies to grow over them. 'Though these inverted trees look somewhat ridiculous at first, they are, when clothed with Ivy, so exceedingly pleasing, and exhibit the trailing character of the Ivy so favourably, that their temporary bareness and peculiarity may be freely submitted to.' Oak stumps were used on steep banks in the pinetum, too, where they threw out a few shoots in summer and were interplanted with bilberries and ferns for picturesque effect.

The form of the stumpery at Biddulph may have been suggested by an archway of tree roots at Bagno, a garden at Steinfort in Westphalia, illustrated in Le Rouge's *Détails des nouveaux jardins à la mode*, though Bateman and Cooke improved on it by concealing most of their rather grotesque structure with plants. They would also have read of the use of stumps as supports for plants in the *Dissertation on Oriental Gardening*, where Sir William Chambers noted that the Chinese placed 'decayed trees, pollards and dead stumps of picturesque form, overspread with moss and ivy' among shrubs and flowers. Maria Louisa Jackson, who lived at Somersal Hall, near Uttoxeter, suggested in *The Florist's Manual* (1822) that 'periwinkle and other running plants will readily grow among mossy trunks, roots, or arms of dead trees; and these thrown carelessly on the ground, and judiciously planted, might form part of the beauty of the garden'. Loudon, in his catalogue of the myriad features of Alton Towers, listed 'old trunks of trees' and 'entire dead trees'.

Bateman was using tree stumps before Cooke first visited Biddulph. In 1841 he wrote to Sir William Hooker: 'I have to thank you and Mr Smith on my own and my gardeners part for the very rich & welcome box of Ferns that you

The plan of the Chinese garden accompanying Edward Kemp's articles in the Gardeners' Chronicle *in 1862. The planting as well as the architectural framework is shown in some detail.*

98

MASSES OF EVERGREENS

WALL OF CHINA

JOSS HOUSE

RUINS OF WALL

MASSES OF WEEPING TREES ON STOCKS

GRASS

GRASS

WALL OF CHINA

IRISH YEWS

MASSES OF EVERGREENS

TUFA

STEPS TO TOWER

TOWER

THE IVY BUSHES

MOUTANS

HIGH CLIFFS

GREAT WALL OF CHINA

TUFA

CHINESE DOOR

TUFA

PINES

BOWLING GREEN

RIDGE

ZIGZAG RAILING

GRASS

SEAT

CHINESE IDOL

THE CHINESE WATERS

YEWS ON HIGH MASSES OF ROCK

FERNS

STEPS

GIGANTIC FROG

TEMPLE

TERRACE

GROTTO

YEWS

FERNS

GROTTO

SUBTERRANEAN PASSAGE

99

have so kindly sent to Knypersley. . . . Mr Dean (my gardener) has already scoured the country for old stumps for their accommodation on which I trust they will find themselves at home.' He was probably using them in the way suggested by Jane Loudon in *The Ladies' Companion to the Flower Garden*: 'Two or three large stools of trees grouped together on a lawn with mould and plants placed in their interstices, form a striking contrast to the smoothness and high art displayed on the general surface of the lawn.' She also suggested the use of roots in something resembling the stumperies which were a speciality of Edward Cooke's. Cooke had stumperies in both his Kensington gardens and at his final home, Glen Andred, and designed stumperies for the gardens of his friends.

Paxton, too, used tree roots and stumps as a setting for plants by the drive-way between the conservatory and the arboretum at Chatsworth: 'From the Conservatory we pass through a rustic arch and find ourselves in a deep cutting of the shale, through which the carriage drive is made, the lofty sides of which are strewed with immense roots and trunks of decayed trees, as if they had been heaped for ages by some convulsion of nature, some of them erect, and the whole of the bank planted solely with British ferns' (William Adam, *Gem of the Peak*). Paxton was probably responsible for a similar feature in the Crystal Palace gardens at Sydenham. Stumperies continued to be made in gardens until rusticity generally fell out of favour.

The stumpery at Biddulph was succeeded by rocks as the path entered China, the most celebrated part of the garden and one of the last notable examples of gardening in the Chinese style. Exotic buildings in a variety of styles, including the Chinese, frequently appeared in the new landscape gardens of the eighteenth century. The earliest Chinese pavilion was built at Stowe, Buckinghamshire, in 1738 and was later moved to Harristown in Co. Kildare, where it still stands. Other early examples were the Chinese house and pagoda at Shugborough, home of the Ansons near Stafford. The Chinese house, which can still be seen, was based on a survey of a building in China by one of Admiral George Anson's officers during his circumnavigation of the world. There were interesting Chinese features in the garden of Richard Bateman (not related to James) at Old Windsor, which was painted by Thomas Robins; while in Lord North's garden at Wroxton Abbey in Oxfordshire there were three Chinese houses and two Chinese bridges.

In 1750 William Halfpenny began the publication of his *Rural Architecture in the Chinese Taste*, with designs of temples, bridges, doors and gates, and there were other similar collections of Chinese designs which might be used in gardens. The architect Sir William Chambers played the major role in promoting the Chinese style, and his influence was felt abroad as well as at home. He had visited Canton while serving with the Swedish East India Company and claimed – not altogether truthfully – that buildings he had sketched there were the basis of *Designs of Chinese Buildings* which appeared in

1757. His best-known building, the ten-storeyed pagoda at Kew, was erected in 1761–2. He published his *Dissertation on Oriental Gardening* in 1772, stating that it was based on his experience in China. This may be partly true, but it owed rather more to the account of the imperial gardens written by a French Jesuit, Jean-Denis Attiret, who had worked as a portrait-painter at the imperial court, and to Chambers's own fantasy. The fashion for Chinese buildings soon spread throughout Europe, and whole villages of Chinese buildings were added to the parks of Wilhelmshöhe, near Cassel, and of Tsarskoye Selo, near St Petersburg.

   The Chinese temple at Biddulph, with its upward-turning eaves, delicately carved woodwork, grebes, dragons and bells, is one of the most successful of European garden buildings in the Chinese style. Cooke prepared designs for it over two summers during visits to Biddulph and he worked at its construction

'China', with its temple, bridge, joss house, dragon parterre and wealth of oriental plants, is the most acclaimed area of the garden and the most difficult for the visitor to find. Illustration from the 1871 sale catalogue.

and decoration with Bateman during the two years which followed. The dragons, which Waterhouse Hawkins sculpted, are similar to those on French 'Chinese' pavilions, among them one in the garden of Claude Baudard de Saint-James at Neuilly, illustrated in Le Rouge's *Détails des nouveaux jardins à la mode*. The very effective transition from the glen to 'China' through the dark, winding tunnel may have been suggested by Robert Fortune's description, in *Wanderings in China*, of the house of a mandarin. At the end of what appeared to be a subterranean passage the garden, 'with its dwarf trees, vases, rock-work, ornamental windows and beautiful flowering shrubs, is suddenly opened to the view'.

Behind the Chinese temple there is another passage in addition to the tunnel from the glen. It leads to a dome-shaped ice-house in a mass of rock-work with a brick-lined circular pit about 8 feet wide and 8 feet deep. This arrangement may have been inspired by the garden of Saint-James at Neuilly, where there was a pavilion placed over an ice-house and near to an underground passage; while in the garden of Cheshunt Cottage, near Theobalds in Hertfordshire, described in the *Gardener's Magazine* in 1839, there was a Chinese temple with a grotto and an ice-house behind it.

OPPOSITE PAGE *The Chinese temple in 1974 after not altogether authentic redecoration.*

BELOW *The giant stone frog in 'China' was based on a model by Waterhouse Hawkins.*

The gilded ox with a solar disc between its horns which gazes across the Chinese waters may have been an echo of the famous bronze ox in the Summer Palace outside Peking. Like the stone frog, the dragons and perhaps the grebes on the roof of the temple, it was the work of Waterhouse Hawkins, the sculptor of the prehistoric animals in the park of the Crystal Palace at Sydenham. There were also 'lions, kymans and other sundry Chinese monstrosities', some of which were probably bought by Cooke for Bateman at auction sales in London. 'Went to Stevens, bought a pair of Urbino lions for Mr B.' Another entry in his diary records the purchase of Chinese kylins. This term should refer to a mythical beast with the head of a dragon, the hooves of a deer, a bushy tail and a single horn, but the word has often been wrongly used for a lion of Fo (Buddha). Lions of Fo came in pairs, the male playing with a ball and the female with a cub, and, since a female survives at Biddulph, it may be that Cooke's 'kylins' were in fact lions.

Though the architectural features are of great interest in 'China', the plants were the most important element here as elsewhere in the garden. At the end of the eighteenth and during the first years of the nineteenth centuries there had been a steady increase in the availability of Chinese plants, thanks to the work of the collectors John Reeves and William Kerr, and by the time Repton advised the 6th Duke of Bedford on his garden at Woburn Abbey, he was able to propose 'the Chinese garden, surrounding a pool in front of the great Chinese pavilion, to be decorated with plants from China . . . such as the hydrangea, aucuba, camellia Japonica'.

Chinese plants were also used in association with Chinese buildings at Leigh Park in Hampshire by Sir George Staunton, whose father, Sir George Leonard Staunton, had taken him on Lord Macartney's Embassy to China in 1792 as page to the ambasssador. Although he was only eleven, he had already studied Chinese and made a great impression on the Emperor. In 1798 he went to Canton with the East India Company and took charge of their factory there in 1816. He visited Peking in the following year. After returning to England in 1820 he bought Leigh Park, where he kept his considerable collection of Chinese books and works of art and created a landscape garden with a lake said to be inspired by a lake in Peking. There was a two-storeyed summerhouse, built in 1826, a bridge and a boathouse, all in the Chinese style and with Chinese inscriptions. The Chinese imperial flag flew over a battery of nine guns on Fort Island, one of three islands in the lake.

Sir George Leonard Staunton had collected plants in China and had built up a considerable herbarium of Chinese specimens, which was to form part of the famous herbarium of the botanist A. B. Lambert. Both his father and Sir Joseph Banks encouraged the young George's early interest in botany, which continued to develop, and he introduced many Chinese plants into the garden at Leigh Park, including some of Robert Fortune's introductions in the 1840s. He had a collection of orchids and was credited with being the first to flower

The surviving golden larch, Pseudolarix amabilis, *in the Chinese garden at Biddulph, one of those introduced by Robert Fortune from China in a Wardian case, may be the oldest in cultivation. The illustration is from* Curtis's Botanical Magazine.

M.S.del. J.N.Fitch lith.

Vincent Brooks Day & Son Ltd imp

L. Reeve & Cᵒ London

Cyrtopodium punctatum in England. Tropical fruit were also produced there – mangoes on a plant supplied by Loddiges, various kinds of passion fruit, white and purple guavas and rose apples. With these interests in common and since they were both Fellows of the Royal Society, it seems probable that Staunton and Bateman would have been acquainted. Staunton may have made suggestions for the Chinese garden at Biddulph, and if the gilded ox at Biddulph *is* an echo of the bronze ox at the Summer Palace, Staunton seems to be Bateman's likeliest source of information, since very few Englishmen had then visited Peking.

Many impressive plants remain in the Chinese garden, but they are only a small proportion of the plants which Kemp saw when he visited Biddulph in 1856 and 1862. Some had been recently introduced from China and Japan by Robert Fortune using Wardian cases, among them the golden larch (*Pseudolarix*

The Japanese anemone, Anemone hupehensis japonica, *one of numerous Fortune introductions which Bateman planted in 'China'.*

OPPOSITE PAGE Skimmia japonica *is thought to have reached Biddulph through the seed supplied by Fortune to the nursery of Standish and Noble in 1852. The illustration is from* Curtis's Botanical Magazine.

2.

3.

4.

5.

1.

6.

amabilis), the Japanese anemone (*Anemone hupehensis* japonica), *Rhododendron* 'Amoenum', *Cryptomeria japonica* 'Sinensis', *Mahonia bealii, Mahonia fortunei, Spiraea japonica* fortunei, *Viburnum plicatum*, various moutan peonies and hostas, a variegated bamboo (*Arundinaria japonica* 'Variegata'), *Cryptomeria japonica* 'Nana', *Skimmia japonica* and *Thujopsis dolabrata*.

One of a pair of golden larches mentioned by Kemp survives, and when Michael Lear and Beverley Woods carried out a botanical survey for the National Trust they found the stump of the other. A ring count showed that it was approximately 127 years old, which pointed to a planting date of about 1855 since it is thought to have died in the early 1980s. Fortune wrote in 1860 that 'all the plants of any size now in England were dug up in the woods of China and sent home in Ward's cases'. Lear and Woods conclude that 'this is an original introduction, probably the oldest in existence in cultivation'. The respective contributions of Fortune and Ward to the Chinese garden at Biddulph were so considerable that it seems unlikely that it would have been attempted without them.

Kemp was impressed by Bateman's use of form and colour in 'China'. 'The most important effects are produced by clustering together masses of spiry plants, such as Irish Yew, or plants with distinct colour, as Golden Hollies.' Purple-leaved varieties of elm (*Ulmus x sarniensis* 'Purpurea'), beech (*Fagus sylvatica* 'Purpurea') and hazel (*Corylus maxima* 'Purpurea') also caught his eye, though these were all surpassed by the red leaves of a Japanese maple (*Acer palmatum* 'Rubrum'), 'perhaps the most effective plant in the collection'. In a talk to members of the Royal Horticultural Society, Bateman said of this tree: 'If seen with an appropriate background – and an appropriate background for this plant when seen out of doors is the sun – nothing can possibly be more beautiful than these leaves. They shine with a brilliant metallic reddish copper transparency that cannot be described.' Bateman particularly liked to mix purple and golden leaves and advocated the use of golden yew, golden holly, golden ivy and golden bramble in such combinations. He supported this advice by demonstrating the effect of placing the leaves of this maple against branches of golden yew. 'Now, contrasting the richer tint with the dark one, how can anything possibly be more beautiful, taking such a background as this, and putting golden yew upon it? And what I can do in this room anyone may do with equal effect out of doors. By simply planting golden yews in the neighbourhood of purple shrubs and trees, you have a great variety of golden tints – a perfect California in short.'

Hostas and yuccas were planted in large groups of mixed species, while other plants which were effectively massed were *Aucuba japonica*, pyracanthas, *Chaenomeles speciosa, Thuja orientalis* 'Aurea', *Weigela florida* and *Weigela coraeensis, Anemone hupehensis* japonica, *Lilium tigrinum*, junipers and *Chamaecyparis thyoides* 'Variegata'. Trees of weeping form included the weeping larch (*Larix x pendula*), the weeping form of purple osier (*Salix*

The Japanese maple, Acer palmatum *'Rubrum', in 'China'. 'If seen with an appropriate background – and an appropriate background for this plant when seen out of doors is the sun – nothing can possibly be more beautiful than these leaves' (Bateman).*

Paulownia tomentosa, *a native of China, was introduced into Britain via Japan in 1834 and was planted in 'China' at Biddulph.*

OPPOSITE PAGE Mutisia decurrens *from* Curtis's Botanical Magazine. *'The brilliant orange flowers glittered like gas jets', Bateman told members of the Royal Horticultural Society in 1866.*

purpurea 'Pendula'), the weeping thorn (*Crataegus monogyna* 'Pendula') and the weeping Japanese pagoda tree (*Sophora japonica* 'Pendula').

'China' lies in remarkable seclusion at the heart of the garden, cut off from the areas which surround it by masses of earth (from the excavation of the lake), rock and dense planting. As a result it is very sheltered, and among plants Kemp was surprised to see growing in the open were *Deutzia gracilis*, *Garrya laurifolia* 'macrophylla', the Assam tea, *Camellia sinensis* and the Chinese orange. Perhaps it was in 'China' that Bateman succeeded with *Mutisia decurrens*. 'The brilliant orange flowers glittered like gas jets. . . . He was happy to be able to inform the meeting', at the Royal Horticultural Society in July 1866, 'that when he left his garden in Cheshire [*sic*] than which a worse climate could hardly be found, it was in flower on a wall where it had never received any protection whatever.' Another plant which performed well at Biddulph was *Trillium grandiflorum*. 'I should not mind going many miles to see the magnificent bushes of this that are at Biddulph Grange in flower. Fancy leaves two feet high and of great strength, every one of which had "set off" a great snow-white flower!' (*Gardener's Magazine*, 1866).

W. Fitch, del et lith.

Vincent Brooks, Imp.

ABOVE *Moutan or tree peony growing at Benthall Hall, a National Trust property in Shropshire, where the Batemans' youngest son, Robert, lived from about 1890 until 1906 and remodelled the garden.*

RIGHT Trillium grandiflorum. *'In marvellous perfection in the highly interesting gardens of Mr Bateman at Biddulph Grange', wrote a correspondent in the Gardener's Magazine in 1866.*

Bateman chose the warmest and most sheltered part of 'China' for a collection of moutan peonies which included Fortune's introductions. He persevered with them for ten years, but they flowered satisfactorily only once and he moved a number of them to the central border of the orchard-house at Knypersley where they flourished.

The hothouses at Knypersley have to be seen as part of the garden at Biddulph. Orchids remained Bateman's major study, while a wide range of tropical and other tender fruits continued to be cultivated there, among them grapes, figs, peaches, nectarines, melons, oranges, lemons, bananas, mangosteens, carambolas, granadillas, kumquats and loquats. In the 1860s there were fourteen hothouses, the largest of them, the orchard-house, measuring 182 feet by 20 feet, and Bateman built an 'ornamental reception house or luncheon saloon of two rooms with portico entrance' in which to entertain fellow enthusiasts who visited his collection. The kitchen garden and orchard were also at Knypersley.

The epiphyte house at Knypersley from James Bateman's Orchidaceae of Mexico and Guatemala. *Bateman continued to grow orchids and tropical fruits at Knypersley after he had moved to Biddulph.*

FIVE

Plants and Gardeners

I t is unfortunate that Bateman's garden records have not survived, for there is no comprehensive information about his sources of plants. Some of them, particularly orchids, came directly from the plant collectors whose expeditions he sponsored. As a Fellow of the Horticultural Society ('Royal' in 1861) he would also have been entitled to a share of the new seeds, plants and cuttings which the Society was receiving from its collectors, notably Robert Fortune.

The Royal Botanic Gardens at Kew were another important source of plants. Details of those sent to Bateman are recorded in the Kew 'Outwards' books and in the correspondence of successive Directors at Kew. The first plants he received were three orchids in 1832. The same correspondence and the Kew 'Inwards' books show that Bateman frequently reciprocated with plants from Knypersley and Biddulph. His requests for plants were pleasantly phrased, as in these two instances to Dr (later Sir) Joseph Hooker: 'You might possibly be disposed – at the same time – to nip off a morsel of one of the Kew plants [a dendrobium] & if the operation is performed with *your own fingers* I will warrant that the bit – be it never so small – shall soon make a plant.' 'Please also to intercede [with Sir William Hooker] in the matter of the new Cypripedium of which when at Kew I saw four plants just received from India. I cannot tell you how I long for a morsel. . . .' Or a request to Sir William for some plants for his wife: 'Mrs Bateman is very anxious that I should do a little begging on her behalf. . . Drynaria musaefolia, D. quercifolia, Neopteris austrice. If you can spare either of them you would make *her* very happy as she has the fern mania very strong indeed upon her at present.'

Bateman would have been given plants, cuttings and seeds by friends and acquaintances with hothouse collections and gardens, but most of the plants at Biddulph Grange would have been bought from nurseries. It seems safe to assume that during the 1840s many would have come from Loddiges', some of them probably on an exchange basis, for Bateman was the source of numerous orchids in the Hackney collection. George Loddiges's handwritten revision of the nursery's 1839 orchid catalogue indicates that 44 of those listed had been obtained from Bateman. No other nursery had introduced so many plants, and Bateman, like George Loddiges, was always anxious to acquire what was new.

Batemani colleyi *from* W. J. Hooker's A Century of Orchidaceous Plants, *1851, named by Dr Lindley to commemorate James Bateman and Thomas Colley.*

Apart from their unrivalled stock of orchids, he would have been drawn to their remarkable arboretum to study the vast range of trees and shrubs they were offering for sale. No doubt he also visited the arboretum at the Abney Park Cemetery at Stoke Newington, which George Loddiges laid out between 1839 and 1841, supplying and organising the planting of some 20,000 trees and shrubs.

There are probably many trees at Biddulph today which originated in Hackney. In their report Michael Lear and Beverley Woods identified a number of trees which they found listed in Loddiges' catalogues but not elsewhere and they consider that oaks and thorns in the pinetum and maples in the arboretum came from the nursery, which may well also have supplied Bateman with cotoneasters, junipers, epimediums, roses, yuccas, phloxes and dahlias.

Bateman also obtained plants from Veitch & Son, who were becoming increasingly well regarded by the middle of the century and were to succeed Loddiges as the most important nurserymen in the country. He was a frequent visitor to their premises in the King's Road. Among other nurseries he would have visited when staying in London, as he often did, were Rollisson's at Tooting, Chandler's at Vauxhall, Hugh Ronald's at Brentford, Henderson's at Paddington and St John's Wood and Hugh Low's at Clapton. Various plants, including rhododendrons, came from Waterer's nursery in Woking, which Bateman visited with Edward Cooke. And, of course, he would not have missed sales of orchids at Stevens's in Covent Garden when he was in town. He also obtained a few plants from nurseries abroad, among them the *Acer negundo* 'Variegatum', which originated in the nurseries of M. Fromane of Toulouse and was awarded a medal by the Empress Eugénie. In a letter to Sir Joseph Hooker Bateman referred to plants he had received from Linden, Belgium's leading orchidist, on condition he did not propagate them.

Plants from Robert Fortune's first journey to China would have reached Bateman through the Horticultural Society, but many plants from Fortune's later visits to China and from his visits to Japan went to the nursery of Standish and Noble at Bagshot in Surrey. It was from them that Bateman obtained *Spiraea japonica* fortunei, some moutan peonies, the golden larch and other Fortune introductions. Standish and Noble also supplied him with some of the important new rhododendrons which Joseph Hooker collected in the Sikkim-Himalaya. They advertised these as hardy in the *Gardeners' Chronicle*, but Bateman, as we have seen, had to give them the protection of glass. He bought two species of callixene from them as well, which did not prove to be as hardy as their catalogue claimed but did well when moved from the garden into the conservatory.

When large quantities of basic plants were required a source nearer home would probably have been preferred. We know from a letter to his brother-in-law, Rowland Egerton-Warburton, that Bateman found good golden hollies near Northwich in Cheshire: 'There was a garden (not exactly a nursery garden) near the turn of the road at Davenham where I bought some very good golden hollies more than ten years ago, & where the people finding the thing paid, said they wd raise some more of the same kind. Generally speaking golden hollies (bright) are not to be had unless you or yr gardener walk the nurseries & pick out the plants *there & then*. If you merely order golden hollies they always send inferior varieties. There are always a few good ones in every nursery but I never saw a large *stock* of the good kinds.'

The most important local nurseryman was William Caldwell of Knutsford, also in Cheshire. The nursery which he controlled dates back to 1759 and still continues today as William Caldwell and Sons Ltd. A remarkable number of their early records have survived, including their day books, with detailed lists of plants supplied to customers for the years 1789–97, 1820–4 and 1828–37, and their cash books for 1798–1818 and 1832–49. We can see from the records of his expenses that William Caldwell made regular journeys to Staffordshire, Shropshire, Wales, Manchester and Warrington visiting customers, and the receipts and the day books show that many of the major gardens in these areas bought plants from him.

This nursery had supplied plants to the parents of both James and Maria Bateman; to her cousin, Sir Philip Grey Egerton, at Oulton Park; and substantial quantities of plants on many occasions to her brother, Rowland Egerton-Warburton, at Arley Hall. James Bateman bought plants from Caldwell in 1842, but no orders appear to have been placed during the following six years, and the cash books and day books for the Batemans' remaining years at Biddulph have not survived.

Bateman must also have visited Frederick Fox's Cliff Vale and Prospect Nurseries at Cheddleton, near Leek in Staffordshire. Plants listed in Fox's 1843 catalogue which might have tempted him were *Fagus sylvatica* 'Atro-rubens', a new variety of purple beech; *Sorbus aucuparia* 'Aurea', a mountain ash with golden leaves; *Taxus baccata* 'Argentea', a silver-striped yew; fifty varieties of *Anemone hortensis*; and *Paeonia officinalis* 'Aurea', a peony with yellow blotches on the leaves. Even nearer home, native plants – ivies, ferns, gorse, heathers, bilberries and hollies – were collected in the surrounding countryside.

Unfortunately there is almost no information about the labour Bateman employed to make the garden and then to maintain it, but we do know that he engaged some very able head gardeners. Outstanding among them was Patrick Neill Don*, who was head gardener at Knypersley in the 1830s and must have had much to do with the early successes Bateman enjoyed with tropical fruits and orchids. He may even have assisted with the *Orchidaceae*, since he was later to edit James Donn's *Hortus Cantabrigiensis* (13th edition, 1845). He belonged to a quite remarkable family of botanists. His father, George Don, was Curator of

*Called after Dr Patrick Neill, Secretary of the Caledonian Horticultural Society, who was a friend of his father.

the Edinburgh Botanical Garden before giving up that post to establish his own nursery. His brother George, after working in the Chelsea Physic Garden, became, as we have seen, a collector for the Horticultural Society, visiting Brazil, the West Indies and Sierra Leone. He was a Fellow of the Linnean Society and published a number of botanical and horticultural works. His brother David was the Linnean Society's Librarian, was elected a Fellow of the Society and became Professor of Botany at King's College, London. A third brother, James Edward Smith Don, was the 1st Earl Amherst's gardener; while a fourth, Charles Lyell Linneus Don, also seems to have worked as a gardener. Patrick Don, after leaving Biddulph, became foreman at Rollisson's nursery in Tooting, noted for its orchids.

In 1841 Elijah Dean, who was then thirty, was head gardener at Biddulph. It is a measure of his standing that he was encouraged to visit the London nurseries in search of new plants. On such a visit in 1845, when the Batemans were in the Isle of Man to benefit Maria Bateman's health, he came back with a gift of orchids from Sir William Hooker at Kew for Knypersley. At Loddiges' he was told that they had been given a cutting of an orchid at Kew which was even better than *Oncidium lanceanum*, and he persuaded Bateman to write to Hooker to beg a cutting.

John Sherratt, praised by Robert Errington for his skill in moving large evergreens and for his management of the orchids, was steward and head gardener at Knypersley in the 1850s and 1860s, a Mr Harding was head gardener at Biddulph in 1859 and a Mr Shoppy in 1862. By 1872, when Biddulph Grange was sold, Sherratt was renting the gardens at Knypersley for £60 a year, and the head gardener at Biddulph was James Stanton. One of Bateman's under-gardeners, Luke Pointon – the census return shows that he was already working for Bateman in 1861 when he was twenty – was later to play a leading part in maintaining Bateman's masterpiece as head gardener to Robert Heath.

Many head gardeners in the nineteenth century worked for employers who knew little about horticulture and were not anxious to assert themselves in the running of their gardens. Those who were engaged at Biddulph, however, found themselves working under the supervision of informed and enthusiastic practical gardeners. 'Mr and Mrs Bateman', wrote Kemp, 'seem to find their chief occupation and amusement in personally directing the progress of the various works.' They were also capable of carrying out any skilled horticultural task which arose.

Letters written by Bateman to Rowland Egerton-Warburton give us interesting glimpses of Bateman's practical gardening skills. In response to a request in 1856 for advice about yew hedges – perhaps Egerton-Warburton was about to plant the hedges which frame the remarkable herbaceous borders at Arley – he counselled: 'If the hedge is not to rise higher than 6–7 ft. . . make a preparation 2 ft deep by taking out the old stuff & putting in new which should

Pieris floribunda. The fine old specimens in the Italian garden were planted by Bateman and still flower profusely in March and April.

be compound of rich soil mixed with rotten leaves & *rotten* manure from the farm-yard, well mixed together.' The plants should be 2 feet apart and then, after about three years, every other plant should be removed for use elsewhere, 'for I will be bound that by that time you will have hatched up some other scheme for which the surplus plants will just come in'. In an exposed position the hedge should be sheltered in winter on the windward side for two seasons, as had been done by Egerton-Warburton's father – Bateman's father-in-law – at Norley Bank. A top dressing of manure should be applied every year, and in the second year 'a few dishes of d--g-water will help matters on amazingly'.

Two years later Egerton-Warburton wrote to him for advice on various matters. In his reply Bateman explained how to construct pillar supports for roses from iron rods and provided a rough sketch of a 'quadripod' support 9 or 10 feet high. For information about varieties to grow on pillars, he suggested that Maria should be consulted, 'as she is very deep in the rose mystery – of which I know nothing'.

Egerton-Warburton also asked about labyrinths, and Bateman replied: 'I don't think you could possibly do better than to turn some of that rather dull (pardon, monsieur!) part of yr grounds near the rose-cum-ilex avenues into an evergreen maze.' Yew should be used, not holly which would become bare at the foot. Four-feet high specimens should be planted on a raised bank with a line of smaller plants at ground level in front of them. 'You will soon have a compact wall 5 ft high, which is high enough for all purposes of perplexity. . . . There is a Hornbeam maze in the Botanic Garden at Manchester which answers well & there is a yew one at Elvaston, which I dare say they would sell *bodily* if you bid handsomely for it, – at all events I never knew Barron [the head gardener] refuse to sell anything yet.'

He advised how to deal with old golden hollies which have grown bare at the base: 'You should plant younkers [young plants] round the skirts of yr aged specimens (having first taken out the old and put in fresh loam) and they will soon form decent petticoats, quite up to the modern fashion.' He also offers some 'unasked advice': 'I don't like yr ilices and would strongly recommend you to substitute Cembra which are of the easiest culture, perfectly hardy, and of a more dignified aspect. . . . You can't make ilices grow equally together & they don't like the knife.' (Fortunately Arley still has its evergreen oaks.) Bateman was writing in Oxford and apologised for a hastily scribbled letter, but he was due to call on the President of Magdalen College to advise on the garden there.

Bateman was as ready to share his garden with others as he was to share his expertise and he welcomed visits by the general public to Biddulph Grange. In 1862 admittance was free between the hours of one and six in the afternoon on the first Mondays of June, July, August and September, and visits were also allowed on any Friday in the year (except Good Friday), when an entrance fee of a shilling was charged, though children accompanied by parents or

Cardiocrinum giganteum. *'The stately Lilium giganteum [as it was then called], at least 9 or 10 feet in height, has the tropical appearance of a Canna or a Musa, and was apparently seeding [at Biddulph] with freedom' (Kemp, 1856).*

120

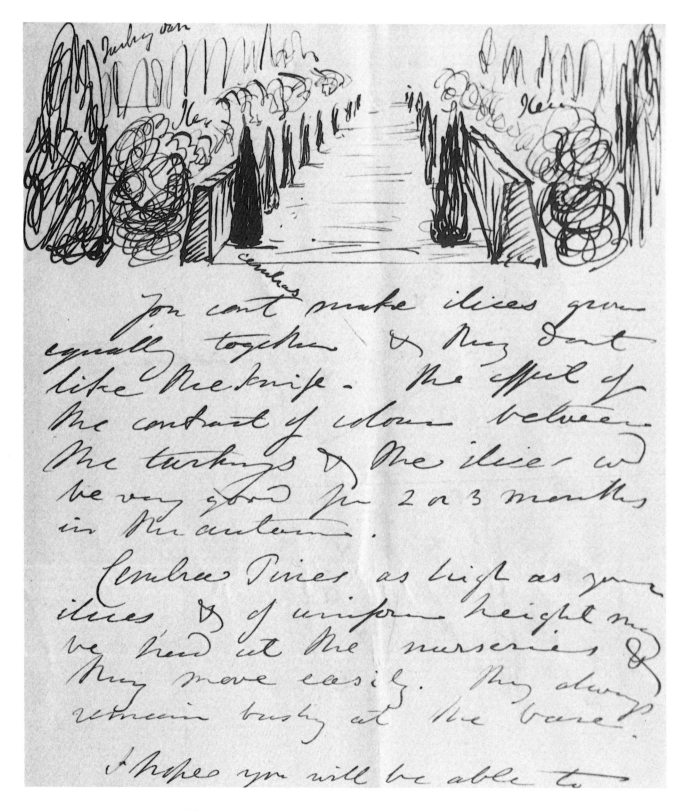

You can't make ilices grow
equally together & they don't
like the knife. The effect of
the contrast of colour between
the turkeys & the ilices will
be very good for 2 or 3 months
in the autumn.

Cembra Pines as high as your
ilices & of uniform height may
be had at the nurseries &
they move easily. They always
remain busty at the base.

I hope you will be able to

guardians were admitted free. 'To foreigners and persons from a distance, who declare themselves unacquainted with the regulations, tickets are issued on other week days.' Under no circumstances were visitors admitted on Sundays. Tickets were obtained at the Church House Inn, and the money received was donated to the Biddulph Old Friendly Society.

Visitors were taken round the garden in groups, and a waiting-room was provided where they could sit until a sufficient number was assembled. For those who preferred to wait in the open air Edward Cooke had designed a seat round the trunk of an American thorn. They were also allowed to visit the museum, which was principally a geological gallery illustrating 'the great geological facts of the globe. On the one side, at about three feet from the ground, a series of specimens, showing the earth's formation, and exhibiting all the various strata in their natural succession, are let into the wall, in a layer about eighteen inches wide; and above this are arranged the animal and vegetable fossils that the respective strata yield. Many rare and elegant examples are here brought together, and as the once-living organisms are placed exactly above the strata from which their remains were taken, the series constitutes at once the most simple and complete lesson in practical geology which could be imagined' (Kemp). There was also a vivarium, a collection of humming-birds and collections of Roman and Central American antiquities. The latter, like the humming-birds, would have been obtained from George Skinner, or perhaps collected by John Bateman, James's eldest son, when he went to Guatemala with Skinner in 1860.

In August 1862 a 'Volunteer Fête' was held at Biddulph Grange. Bateman invited the Volunteers (forerunners of the Territorials) of North Staffordshire and Cheshire to visit the garden, providing them with railway tickets and arranging for a special train to carry them along the mineral branch line to Biddulph. Military bands played in the garden, and James and Maria Bateman each gave prizes of 10 guineas for the winners of marksmanship competitions. Visitors were invited to use the quoits ground, bowling green and fives court, and there was a bazaar. 'A powerful body of Police will be in attendance, but Mr. BATEMAN trusts that their interference will not be required, and that all persons attracted to the Fête will deem it due to the occasion and to themselves, to behave in a becoming and orderly manner.' Thousands of visitors attended, paying half-a-crown for admission before 2 pm and a shilling afterwards. Almost £250 was raised towards the building of the church – Christ Church – which Edward Cooke had designed, at Biddulph Moor.

In a letter to his brother-in-law, Rowland Egerton-Warburton of Arley Hall, Cheshire, James Bateman offered advice on the planting of a complex avenue. 'You can't make ilices [evergreen oaks] grow equally together & they don't like the knife. The effect of the contrast of colour between the turkeys & the ilices would be very good for 2 or 3 months in the autumn.

Cembra Pines as high as your ilices and of uniform height may be had at the nurseries and they move easily. They always remain bushy at the base.'

SIX

Beyond the Garden

Although many of the seventeen hundred or so acres of the Knypersley and Biddulph Grange estates were in the hands of the tenants who farmed them, substantial areas were retained by the family for sport and recreation and two of these areas formed interesting landscape extensions of the garden. The first was the old deer park which had been disparked in 1795 but was restocked by James Bateman in 1859. In 1867 there were about eighty head of fallow deer in the 108 acres, enclosed by a high stone wall and a wire fence. This is an area of wild beauty, now part of the Greenway Bank Country Park, with steep hills crowned by enormous rocks. Many of the pines and other trees must have been planted by John or James Bateman.

Two features of great interest in the park are the Gawton stone and well, both mentioned by Robert Plot in his *History of Staffordshire* (1686). The former looks like a cromlech but was probably formed when a very large rock became detached from the mass above and came to rest on three others. According to tradition the space under this enormous capstone served as a hermitage for many years. In the 1871 sale catalogue it was described as a 'Druidical Cromlech . . . and evidently a Sacrificial or Sacred Structure, of intense Archaeological Value'. On 13 October 1861 Cooke recorded that it was excavated in the presence of some of the members of the British Association, who were visiting Biddulph Grange after a meeting in Manchester. He does not say what was found.

The well is set in a grove of yew trees and enclosed by a stone wall. The water flows first into a circular basin and then into two sunken stone baths which are now silted up. When Plot wrote his history the water was reputed to cure the king's evil*, and there was said to be the base of an ancient stone cross here in 1871.

In the 1820s a new reservoir, Knypersley Pool, was formed on the western boundary of the park to improve the water supply to James Brindley's Trent and Mersey Canal. It augmented the adjacent Serpentine, a reservoir made for the same purpose in the 1780s, and has the appearance of a natural lake, adding considerably to the beauty of the park. The river Trent, which rises nearby,

*A disease affecting the lymphatic gland.

flows swiftly through a deep valley to feed Knypersley Pool, while a leat made in 1780 draws off water from the river and flows through the park to fill the Serpentine. John Bateman responded to the appeal of the new reservoir by building a miniature sandstone castle near the shore in 1828 and the leat was made to flow round it to represent a moat. This feature, which survives, was known as the warder's tower and later provided a home for one of James Bateman's gamekeepers, from where he could watch over the wild duck and snipe on the water as well as the deer in the park. There seems to have been some kind of collection of interesting objects in the building, for Cooke recorded that he sheltered there with John Bateman and 'examined curiosities during a heavy shower'. The young James Bateman made a lithograph of the warder's tower, of which there is a proof in the William Salt Library in Stafford inscribed 'drawn on stone by James Bateman'. The warder's tower is also one of the four views, probably all the work of Bateman, reproduced on the Spode plate made to commemorate his twenty-first birthday (see p. 63). The building and the bridge nearby may have been the work of James Trubshaw, since he

James Bateman's drawing of the warder's tower in the deer park at Knypersley, which was built by his father, John Bateman, in 1828 and may have been designed by James Trubshaw.

was consulted by the Trent and Mersey Canal Company about the construction of the reservoir. He did some work on St Lawrence's Church for John Bateman, as did his son Thomas.

The deer park was linked with Biddulph Grange by a private carriage drive some two miles long which had been laid out at considerable expense. Starting by the lime avenue, its course ran sometimes across stretches of open field, sometimes through new plantations, passing close to the massively impressive Wickenstone rocks and a small sandstone lodge designed by Cooke before descending to the shore of the pool. This was some of the best scenery in North Staffordshire, and it would have made an idyllic excursion on a fine day in the Batemans' britzska.

The second landscape extension of the garden followed Bateman's acquisition of Biddulph Old Hall in 1863. This romantic ruin, the remains of a substantial and attractive stone building of the sixteenth century, was the home of the Biddulph family. Supporters of the king in the Civil War, they were besieged for three months by Parliamentary forces here and were eventually forced to surrender when bombarded by Roaring Meg, a cannon brought from Stafford. The local population, looking for salvage, finished the work started by Roaring Meg, leaving only the shell of the building. Bateman saw that the Old Hall would make a marvellous feature to terminate a vista. It also offered another opportunity for archaeological research, and on 12 August 'all went up to the ruins and with 40 men commenced digging in all parts & traced out some of the walls and floors of tiles'.

The land Bateman acquired with the Old Hall extended to his boundary and included a long stretch of dingle, or clough, with a waterfall, a stream, a mill house and cottage – all appropriate features for a picturesque walk. The route Bateman devised followed a wooded stream from the Grange and then passed under a lane (Fold Lane) through a stone-lined tunnel (still there though blocked at one end). It continued through a plantation to the dingle, where it again followed a stream, passing from one side to the other across rustic bridges. After three-quarters of a mile, it turned into the main avenue of the sixteenth-century garden with the magnificent ruin suddenly revealed at the far end. (The near end of the avenue had been closed with a bank of earth in order to preclude a premature and less effective view.) And from the ruin there were views of the Cheshire plain, the surrounding hills and Mow Cop, an eighteenth-century folly built as an eye-catcher to be seen from Rode Hall, home of the Batemans' friends the Wilbrahams.

James and Maria Bateman were both deeply religious. Maria's piety is revealed in a letter she wrote to her son Rowland, expressing her joy at his decision to devote his life to the church: 'Treasure of my heart! and apple of my eye! . . . It will be a gratification to you to know that this time twenty-one years ago I was Beseeching the Gracious Giver of all good things to accept for His special service my new-born babe. . . .'

The picturesque walk to the ruins of Biddulph Old Hall. The Batemans' son Robert (right) and his wife Caroline (on the bridge) lived for a time in the house by the ruins.

127

James, an evangelical anglican, sold his first collection of orchids (he quickly assembled a second) as a contribution towards the cost of building the church of St John the Evangelist at Knypersley, he built the church and parsonage at Biddulph Moor and he was patron of the Church of St Lawrence at Biddulph. The incumbents of all three churches were frequently entertained at the Grange. James himself was an active local preacher, and at least two of his sermons were published. They make rather heavy reading. Like many of his contemporaries, he believed that Rome was iniquitous, that Darwin had got it all wrong and that the millennium was at hand and would put everything right. It was as natural to him to bring religion into his botanical writings as it was for George Loddiges. In the introduction to the *Monograph of Odontoglossum*, 1864–74, he took issue with Charles Darwin (whom he had provided with orchids for his research) and his supporters, challenging Darwin's use of orchids to support his theories and explaining the thinking, as he saw it, behind the Creation. 'To the believer, however, the problem is not hard to solve. Ferns and other flowerless plants came early in the Divine programme, because the coal, into which they were ultimately to be converted, had need to be long accumulating for the future comfort and civilisation of our race; while the genesis of Orchids was postponed until the time drew near when Man, who was to be soothed by the gentle influence of their beauty, was about to appear on the scene. . . .'

In a lecture on orchids requiring cool conditions to members of the Royal Horticultural Society in 1864, he suggested that the day was rapidly approaching when there would be no new plant species left to collect, and 'our Lindleys and Reichenbachs, our Benthams and Hookers will find their occupation gone'. Clever theories about natural selection would not produce new species. However, those who had studied 'a higher philosophy' knew that the situation would be saved by divine intervention. 'When the appointed hour shall have struck, that voice so mighty in operation shall be heard once more, and the solemn words "Behold, I make all things new" will kindle into life ten thousand forms of animal and vegetable life, and change as in a moment, the whole face of the world.'

Religious prejudice lay at the root of Bateman's objection to hybrids, for he regarded the hybridisation of plants as tampering with the work of God. Of the effect of hybridising rhododendrons he wrote: 'The original forms will inevitably disappear from our gardens, and nowhere, but in their native Himalayas, will the species be seen as they started into being at the fiat of the Almighty.' Harry Veitch had been puzzled by Bateman's reaction to hybrids: 'Mr Bateman is such a kind-hearted, genial gentleman that many a time I have asked myself why, when he came into my houses, he used to act in such an extraordinary manner when he saw a hybrid.' This was said by Veitch at a meeting in 1885 when he gave a paper on the hybridisation of orchids. Bateman was called upon to propose a vote of thanks. His views had mellowed by then, and he explained how he had come to hold them: 'I am sure that he [Veitch], and Mr Dominy [Veitch's hybridizer] also, will know and appreciate the effort it costs me to make this proposal, for I have been brought up with the very strongest abhorrence of hybridizers. (Laughter) . . . My first Orchid-growing friend was Mr Huntley. When I paid Mr Huntley a visit at his snug rectory in Huntingdonshire, he pointed out to me his cacti and his Orchids, and said, "I like those plants, in fact they are the only plants I grow, because those fiends (meaning the hybridizers) cannot touch them". (Laughter) You must make a little allowance for a botanist, for hybridizers do give botanists a lot of trouble – (laughter) – but, however strong my prejudices were, I must confess that when I saw such plants as the cattleya downstairs, if I was not converted, I was, at all events, what amounts to the same thing, shut up. . . .'

It has been argued that Bateman's religious beliefs were the main force behind the garden at Biddulph, which, 'by evoking vanished and alien civilizations, served as an affirmation that the millennium was coming' (Brent Elliott, *Victorian Gardens*). While religion was an important factor throughout Bateman's life, it is difficult to gauge to what extent the garden was created as an expression of faith and how far it was the product of self-indulgence. His conviction that the millennium was close at hand was based on the *Book of Revelation*, in which, he wrote, 'all the chief events that were to befall the Church and world are depicted with higher than human art'. In the *Book of Revelation*, where the dragon represents Satan, we read that 'three unclean spirits like frogs come out of the mouth of the dragon, and out of the mouth of the beast, and out of the mouth of the false prophet' (XVI, 13). This passage was quoted by Bateman in a religious pamphlet. Is his Chinese garden, with its dragons, stone frog and gilded ox, less idyllic than it seems? But if Biddulph Grange was intended primarily as a religious statement, it is surprising that he kept its message to himself. Evangelists are not usually reticent about good news, but there is nothing in Edward Kemp's articles to suggest that he was made aware of the garden's religious significance; nor is there any hint of it in Edward Cooke's diary.

In evoking past ages and distant lands Biddulph Grange is in the tradition of what have been called 'world image' gardens. It is a tradition which goes back to Hadrian's Villa on his estate at Tivoli near Rome in the second century. Having visited every part of the Roman Empire, Hadrian sought to create echoes of the places which had impressed him, including a portico in imitation of the Poikile in Athens, a temple of Serapis and a canal like those at Canope near Alexandria, a vale of Tempe to represent Thessaly, as well as the Elysian fields, which he hoped to visit later. Bateman would almost certainly have visited Tivoli. Eighteenth-century English gardens of similar character include Stowe, with its classical temples and ruins, gothic temple, temple of British worthies, St Augustine's cave, Egyptian pyramid, Chinese house and Elysian fields; Sir William Chambers's Kew; and Shugborough. Perhaps the most

The Chinese house at Shugborough, built in 1747, is said to have been based on a survey of a building in Canton by one of Admiral George Anson's officers.

comprehensive 'world image' garden was the Jardin de Monceau in Paris, which was designed in the 1770s by Louis Carrogis, called Carmontelle, for the anglophile Louis Philippe Joseph d'Orléans, who became the Duc d'Orléans in 1785. As Philippe-Egalité he voted for the death of the king in 1793, only to follow him to the scaffold later in the same year. The extraordinary collection of garden features at Monceau included a Chinese entrance gate, a Chinese bridge, an Egyptian pyramid, an Italian vineyard, a Dutch windmill, a Turkish pavilion, two Turkish tents, a 'ruined' temple of Mars, a Tartar tent and a minaret, with servants, dressed as Tartars and Hindus, required to lead animals brought from Africa and Asia. The head gardener was a Scot, Thomas Blaikie, while most of the plants for the garden were supplied by the Hammersmith nursery of James Lee, whose descendants inherited a very fine set of hand-painted buttons with views of Monceau, a token, no doubt, of the Duke's esteem.

At the Désert de Retz, at Chambourcy near Paris, the architectural features led the visitor through the history of civilisation; while at Hohenheim, near

Stuttgart in Württemberg, the ruling Duke Carl Eugen (a customer of Conrad Loddiges) laid out an 'English' village with buildings in Roman, gothic and Turkish styles and an American garden of rare plants. He was much influenced by a visit to Kew in 1776, where he admired the exotic buildings – the pagoda, the mosque and the 'ruined' Roman tower – designed by Chambers.

Further afield, in January 1774 the Polish connoisseur and amateur architect August Moszynski presented King Stanislas II Poniatowski with his manuscript entitled 'Essay on English Gardening'*, with a description and plan of a garden prepared with the help of the architect Szymon Bogumil Zug. Though this garden did not materialise, it is of great interest. The many garden features proposed by Moszynski included a lantern of Diogenes, temples of Aeolus, Bacchus, Flora, Diana and Pan, a Druids' sacred grove, an elysium of Polish worthies, a rocky Chinese eminence with a pavilion, and a representation of Sicily with an amphitheatre and with a lake featuring a floating island planted with fruit trees. A model of Vesuvius was designed to smoke and rumble during the day and to 'erupt' at night with the aid of fireworks placed inside the crater. A grotto was to lead to a cavern inside the volcano where four giant cyclopean automatons hammered away at Vulcan's forge. (In 1772 Chambers had described the alleged use of artificial volcanoes in Chinese gardens, and a 'volcano' was constructed some years later in the park at Wörlitz, near Dessau, in Upper Saxony.) Moszynski's plan also included recently discovered and more primitive parts of the world, fictional as well as real, for he proposed to recreate the island of Tahiti with shelters formed from artificial banana and banian trees; an Indian dwelling; and the habitation of Robinson Crusoe.

The 15th Earl of Shrewsbury's Alton Towers in the Churnet valley in Staffordshire is a good early nineteenth-century English example of a 'world image' garden. The house itself, then called Alton Abbey, represented the Middle Ages, while the garden features included a gothic prospect tower, a Tudor lodge, a two-tiered stone circle recalling Stonehenge, a Greek temple, numerous statues of Roman gods and mythological figures, a Swiss cottage and a Dutch garden. There was also a Chinese pagoda and bridge, and an Indian cave-temple carved out of sandstone and inscribed, according to Loudon, with hieroglyphics.

All these gardens, apart from Moszynski's unrealised scheme, would have been known to James Bateman, but the idea for Biddulph Grange may well have been first suggested by James Main's 'Outlines of a Plan for the Formation of a Classical Garden', which appeared in the *Gardener's Magazine* in 1831, in the same issue as the article on rock-work. Main proposed the creation of a national garden divided into five areas 'representing the five zones of the terraqueous globe' – the Arctic, the Antarctic, the torrid and the north and south temperate – each appropriately planted.

The area representing the Arctic would be small and would be entered

The Chinese pagoda, the best-known of William Chambers's garden buildings at Kew.

*Based on F.-de-P. Latapie's French translation of Thomas Whately's *Observations on Modern Gardening*.

'through an arch of rustic rock-work, formed of the native rock of the arctic circle, or from as near to it as can be brought home by the northern whalers. In the interstices of this structure let every plant indigenous to the hyperborean shores be planted.' Further ornament could be provided by 'whale bones, testacea, horns of the elk, &c'.

The principal feature in the torrid zone was to be a mosque, presumably partly of glass, with a pyramid behind it to act as a chimney. Here there would be a collection of tropical fruits and flowers, palms, plantains and 'all the vegetable children of the sun'. There would be tropical plants outside, too, in the summer, but they would be backed by a permanent planting of pines and cedars disguised as palms – 'kept pruned up to form palm-like heads'.

China, where Main had worked as a plant collector, was to be represented by a Chinese conservatory. 'Its structure, ornaments, colouring and its beautiful plants both within and without, wholly Chinese; a pagoda at each corner behind, serving as chimneys, will mark its character, and enrich the scene. . . . In this, not only Chinese shrubs, but also trees which are equally beautiful, may be brought to a perfection never seen in this country.'

At Biddulph there were echoes of Greece and Rome in the house, Chinese, Egyptian and Roman architectural elements in the garden, the ruin of an Elizabethan mansion to terminate a picturesque walk and what was thought to be a prehistoric burial chamber in the deer park, while almost every part of the world was represented in the plants growing in the garden and under glass. In addition the museum contained antiquities from Rome, Central America and India, humming-birds from Guatemala and a remarkable geological gallery.

Few 'world image' gardens were laid out after Biddulph Grange; but at Sir Frank Crisp's late nineteenth-century Friar Park, in Oxfordshire, there was a medieval garden, an Elizabethan garden, a French garden, a Dutch garden, a Boccaccio garden, a Japanese garden and a rock garden in the form of a model of the Matterhorn; while at Iford Manor, in Wiltshire, in the early twentieth century, Harold Peto made a Japanese garden and arranged Italian, French, German and Byzantine architectural features and sculpture on existing eighteenth-century terraces.

Other more ephemeral collections of gardens in national styles have been made for international exhibitions and for garden festivals. At the International Garden Festival in Stoke-on-Trent in 1986, on the site of the once rural Etruria Hall estate of Josiah Wedgwood, there were English gardens of just about every period, a Dutch garden, a Norwegian garden, a Kenyan village and Turkish tents, while China was represented by a willow-pattern garden, a public house called the China Garden and an evocation of the Chinese garden at Biddulph Grange created by the Staffordshire Moorlands District Council with the help of pupils from Biddulph High School.

The watch-tower, which offers a commanding view of 'China' at Biddulph, was originally armed with two cannon!

133

SEVEN

Changing Fortunes

After the publication of the last of Kemp's 1856 articles in the *Gardeners' Chronicle* Bateman wrote to the editor to emphasise the extent of his indebtedness to Edward Cooke, 'to whose ever-ready pencil and inexhaustible invention my gardens, I am well aware, owe their chief attractions. With Mr Cooke's skill as a landscape-painter the public is abundantly familiar, but it is not so generally known that he occasionally forsakes his studio to practise his craft of a landscape gardener. In this capacity he has helped me through so many difficulties, and enabled me to realise so many, but for him, impracticable conceptions, that I feel naturally anxious at once to confirm my own obligations to him, and to point out the quarter from whence others also may hope to derive the like assistance.'

Apart from his work in the garden Cooke also designed the church and parsonage at Biddulph Moor, the Knypersley pinfold (see p. 70), the gates to the park, a well, improvements to the Church House Inn, which then stood by the church, some cottages and a laundry. For Bateman's house he designed a tower-chimney, the conservatory-corridor and its balcony, and a new drive with an 'Elizabethan' lodge. His ornamental stone entrance wall with a drinking fountain and seats, conveying 'at once a kindly and hospitable impression', carried the inscription: 'For the refreshment of weary travellers. May God speed them on their way. J.B.' When this drive was later replaced the ornamental wall and drinking fountain were moved to their present position on the corner of Congleton Road and Fountain Court.

Although Biddulph Grange was Edward Cooke's most important commission, he helped to design a number of other gardens during the years he was visiting Biddulph. In 1851, at Betteshanger, the home of Sir Walter James near Deal in Kent, he made plans for a large new garden in place of an orchard and remodelled the stumpery. At Broomhill near Tunbridge Wells, the home of Alderman David Salomons*, he made plans for lodges and terraces and suggested improvements to the garden between 1852 and 1856. At Kiddington Hall in Oxfordshire in 1856–7 he planned a new terrace, a lodge and a Chinese

*Later Sir David Salomons, Member of Parliament, Lord Mayor of London and campaigner for the rights of Jews.

Cooke's Grotesque Animals, *with drawings similar to these, was published in 1872.*

These oddities, from fancy drawn,
May surely raise the question,
Will DARWIN say – by
Chance they're formed,
Or 'Natural Selection' ?

When Cooke was invited to stay with friends or with his patrons he frequently took these and other drawings with him to amuse his hosts and their guests.

QUALIS VITA FINIS ITA.

CHIMERA DIRE!

SPERO ET PROGREDIOR.

SPES ALIT AGRICOLAM.

conservatory and repositioned the greenhouses and forcing-pits for Henry Gaskell, as well as suggesting alterations to the dovecote, the Roman tower and the waterfall. For Herbert Field of Ashurst Park near Tunbridge Wells he 'laid out the new building East End of house and Loggie and part of garden' in 1856 and returned in the following year to work at the rockery and a bridge and spent several days on the stumpery: 'At work all day with 25 men, building up huge stumps and planting on them.' 'Very busy all day fixing huge stumps and planting Cryptomerias and other shrubs.' He planned a terrace and steps for Herbert Field's son, John, living nearby at Dornden. In 1856 he was also employed at Lady Nevill's Dangstein, near Midhurst in Sussex, where he 'made suggestions for altering the drive and other parts of the grounds, Pinetum and Rosary etc . . . made plans for new garden terraces . . . made designs for cottage and parts of garden'. There was a notable collection of orchids at Dangstein, and Bateman and Cooke went there together to stay as guests in 1862.

In the 1850s Cooke made another garden for himself, when, only six years after moving to The Ferns in Victoria Road, he moved again, this time to 9 Hyde Park Gate South, which he also called The Ferns. His gardens at both these addresses were later described in the *Gardeners' Chronicle* as 'models of what small town gardens might be made by one who combined artistic power of grouping and genuine love of plants'.

Work on the new garden began almost a year before the move and continued for as long afterwards. In September 1854 there were as many as seventeen men at work, transferring hollies, yews, thuyas, cypresses and cedars from the old garden to the new, as well as stumps, stones, chalk and logs. During a visit to Biddulph in October 1855 he had gone 'with old Mr Bateman to the lake to see the stumps dug out for me', and two months later 'a van came bringing a quantity of stumps from Mr Bateman. One huge one 14 Cwt. was hoisted over the wall.' Bateman also sent oak branches for the stumpery, and more stumps were bought from Kew Gardens. There were loads of peat, gravel and sandstone, and 'five and a half tons of Tufa came in van in morning and it was pitched outside'. Slates were delivered to pave the fernery. On 17 August 1854, following the removal of Loddiges' stock to Sydenham, Cooke attended a sale at the nursery of 'Old Materials, Hothouses, pipes, Columns, tanks &c. I bought a Tank of iron and part of a slate tank. Collected a quantity of seedlings and young Palms. Took tea with Mrs Loddiges.' As we have seen, Conrad Loddiges, George's son, must have continued to garden privately, if not professionally, and a year later he 'sent van with Camellias and ferns – and took back my orchids to arrange and peat afresh'. At Biddulph Cooke 'went with Mrs Bateman along the borders and she dug me up some of all her choice herbacea'. His friend John Hillersdon sent water lilies and a considerable quantity of wild heaths, and there were gifts of plants from Redleaf, from Thomas Gambier Parry of Highnam Court in Gloucestershire, and from

Nathaniel Ward. Plants were also supplied by the Fulham nurseries of Osborne's and Dancer's, from Masters' in Canterbury and from Anthony Waterer's Knap Hill nursery in Surrey.

Rock-work in the garden was constructed by James Pulham and his men, who worked there at intervals over a period of eighteen months. Pulham was a very successful manufacturer of artificial rock-work, which he produced by pouring cement over mounds of brick and clinker and then shaping them to resemble boulders. The result was sometimes so effective that experts were deceived. There is a good example in Battersea Park in London, and a number of others have survived, including one as far afield as Gisselfeld in Denmark. Cooke had been impressed by Pulham's extensive rock-work in a mixture of real and artificial stone at Highnam Court, which he visited in 1854, and 'made sketches about the Rocky parts of the Winter garden'. Real as well as artificial stone must have been used at The Ferns, where Pulham worked on the terrace, the rockery, the 'rocky pool' and rock-work in the hothouses.

Considerable effort went into constructing and planting the stumpery, which was probably much larger than its predecessor at Victoria Road, and there was also a 'wildery' and a bog for water plants. Garden ornaments and furniture included 'mushroom' seats, like those at Redleaf to which Jane Loudon had taken exception: 'To take off the harshness of this line [the stone walk across the lawn], Mr Wells has introduced some exceedingly ugly seats in the shape of gigantic toadstools, which are certainly a much greater deformity than that which they are intended to conceal.' By the end of August 1855, though the work was not finished, Cooke and his family were ready to receive guests. 'After tea capital game of bowls by moonlight – candles for Jacks. After supper danced in drawing room . . . all left at 2. Garden illuminated, superb moon.'

Cooke's career as a painter continued to flourish, and in 1865 he decided to move out of London when he found the ideal site for a house near Groombridge on the Kent and Sussex border. Here there were splendid rocks on and just below the surface with views to Harrison's rocks across the valley. The construction of the railway line from Tunbridge Wells to Uckfield with a station at Groombridge was a vital factor in Cooke's decision, since it brought London much nearer. His first intention was to design the house himself. He bought a copy of Robert Kerr's *The Gentleman's House*, a comprehensive guide for designers of country houses, and he discussed the plans he had made with the architect Decimus Burton, who 'gave me hints'. He also showed his plans to James Bateman, who, in April 1866, was one of the first to be taken to Groombridge to see the site, and together they determined the position of the house. In May Cooke decided to ask the architect Norman Shaw to take over the planning of the house. 'Got a new plan from Norman Shaw & a letter. Replied (with objections). . . .' When the work started a time capsule was placed in the foundations: 'We laid first stone with bottle of documents and

capped it with another huge stone at four o'clock.'

Rocks were the major element in the garden at Glen Andred, as the new house was called, and Cooke wasted no time in uncovering those which lay below the surface and in rearranging them. He recorded progress in his diary: 'Tested depth of rocks, made plans. . . Excavating and blasting. . . Men getting up the big stones by Punnetts 3 horses. . . Arranged rocks in Rock Vale. . . moved the huge stone in front of the Dolmen and made the hole through. . . Also deepened Crinkum. . . Heaved over huge rock of 10 tons from top of Scotland. . . Developing stone in Rhodo: Grove, deepening fissures, forming steps. . . .' 'If [the rocks] would not show themselves he made them do so. With a long probe he probed the soil around and between the buried rocks, and then scooped away the sand with a diligence *proprio manu*, till bold bluffs, mountain gorges, wooded ravines,with limpid rivulets trickling between, rewarded his exertions. Here was fit resting place for Ferns, for alpines, for aquatics, for anything that would grow.' (*Gardeners' Chronicle*, 1880)

Cooke bought many plants for Glen Andred, most of them from Veitch & Sons. He now looked to Harry Veitch for the sort of help he had once received from George Loddiges. Veitch went to Groombridge more than once to discuss Cooke's plans for the garden and what plants would be needed, and he sent his men to help with planting and pruning. They were also responsible for removing plants from The Ferns to Glen Andred. When Cooke visited the nursery at Coombe Wood in Surrey he was taken there in Harry Veitch's phaeton. The planting of hollies, yews, deodars, Wellingtonias, cedars, conifers in general, heaths, apples, pears, plums, mulberries, walnuts, vines, asparagus, sea kale and artichokes is recorded in the diary.

Glen Andred was, and still is, a wilder, more natural garden than Biddulph Grange, but, as at Biddulph, there was considerable variety and each part of the garden was given a picturesque name suggesting its distinct character. Two areas, Loddigesia and Wardian Valley, commemorated old friends. Harry Veitch was taken on a grand tour of the garden during a visit in 1869. 'After Breakfast went with Harry Veitch all round by Arboretum and stumpery, Ward's Rock and Mount, Glen, Eagle Rock, Scotland, Crinkum Crankum, Wilderness, Bello Squardo, lawn and back to lunch at 1 p.m.' There was also a 'Polyody', a 'Druids' Dell', a 'Bosky' and, after a visit to the Northumberland home of Sir William Armstrong, where bare moors had been planted with vast numbers of conifers, rhododendrons and alpines, a 'Cragside'. Much of the last fifteen years of Cooke's life – he died in 1880 – were spent on improving his grounds.

During his visit to Biddulph in September 1866 Cooke had shown his plans to Bateman and 'went with him all over the Garden jotting down the names of Conifers and plants etc. . . . Worked with Mr B over plans in evening, of my own grounds.' In July 1868 Bateman was the first guest to stay at Glen Andred, and during this visit he discussed with Cooke the possibility of renting The Ferns in Hyde Park Gate South. A few days later he wrote agreeing to take it.

The Batemans intended to spend half of each year at The Ferns, hoping that Maria's bronchitis would improve if she could avoid Biddulph in the winter. They were already frequent visitors to London where James regularly attended meetings at the Royal Horticultural Society and was a familiar figure at the leading nurseries. Members of the Society looked forward to the lectures he gave from time to time on Tuesday afternoons, and in a tribute to him in the *Gardeners' Chronicle* he was said 'to have more nearly realised the ideal of the popular lecturer . . . than anyone before or after'.

Many of his lectures were about orchids, usually illustrated by plants from Knypersley. At these meetings there were also exhibitions of plants and members were awarded certificates for outstanding specimens. Bateman had given a gold medal for the exhibitor awarded the greatest number of certificates for orchids and on 5 June 1866 he presented this to Veitch's Exotic Nursery in the King's Road for their successes in 1864 and 1865. (Nineteen years later Bateman was to be awarded the Veitch Memorial Medal.) One of the orchids exhibited by Bateman on that occasion, a cut specimen of *Dendrobium wardianum*, was awarded a first-class certificate. Nectarines from Knypersley were also on show.

When the subjects of his lectures were edible Bateman liked to give the Fellows and their friends an opportunity of sampling them. During a lecture on the dwarf banana, *Musa cavendishii*, a large bunch was distributed among the audience, and on another occasion he brought some passion fruit, 'the fruit of *Passiflora edulis* that the visitors might taste – a privilege he seldom enjoyed himself, so fond of them were his family. The proper way to eat them was like

Edward Cooke's painting of the garden at Glen Andred. 'Hounds all through our garden and Huntsmen following', he wrote in his diary on 11 April 1871.

an egg, with or without sugar according to taste.' After a lecture on orchids, orchis tea was available for tasting, while cigars made from orchid leaves cased in tobacco leaves were exhibited, lent by the museum at Kew.

Bateman continued to write about orchids. He had provided the descriptions of the orchids and usually the specimens of the orchids themselves which were illustrated in *Curtis's Botanical Magazine* under the editorships of the Hookers. The volume for 1837 was dedicated to Bateman as a tribute to his *Orchidaceae*, 'a work of which it is hard to say whether the beauty of the subjects represented, the execution of the figures, or the taste and judgement displayed in the typographical department is most to be admired'. After the death of Sir William, Bateman explained to Joseph Hooker the arrangement he had had with his father and expressed his readiness to continue: 'The understanding 'twixt yr poor Father & myself was that until I was dismissed I was to provide the Orchids (description & all) for the Bot. Mag., he telling me through Fitch [see below] if there were anything at Kew that he specially wanted to be figd. I am quite willing to go on, so long as you are satisfied with me, but never be in the least afraid of telling me of anything you wish to be done or left undone – or even discharging me altogether.'

Using the nom-de-plume Serapis, he wrote a series of articles for the *Gardeners' Chronicle* in 1862 and 1863 on the history of orchid cultivation in England. In 1864 he published a small booklet, *A Guide to Cool-Orchid Growing*, and in the same year he began publication of his *Monograph of Odontoglossum*. The sixth and final part came out ten years later. In each part there were five colour plates by the flower painter Walter Hood Fitch, whom Sir William Hooker had discovered apprenticed to a firm of calico designers in Glasgow. Fitch provided the drawings for Hooker's *A Century of Orchidaceous Plants* (1851), the subjects for which were selected from plants which had appeared in the *Botanical Magazine*. After the death of Hooker Bateman followed his work with *A Second Century of Orchidaceous Plants* (1867), again with illustrations by Fitch. Bateman had a high regard for Fitch's work, though he felt he had one weakness: 'Fitch's only fault is this disposition to flatter his subjects – just as Sir Thos. Lawrence did his ladies.'

Another landmark in Bateman's career was the acceptance of his scheme for the layout of the University Museum Parks in Oxford. In February 1863 he called on Cooke with plans he had prepared, and Cooke 'worked over' them. There were further consultations during the weeks which followed. Bateman sent a copy of the final plan, with its ornamental walks, avenue of Wellingtonias, plantings of trees which 'will produce the most striking effect in Spring and Autumn', bathing place, bridge over the Cherwell and cricket ground, to Sir William Hooker, hoping he would write to the Park Delegates in its support. Not long afterwards he wrote again to thank him for his help: 'The delegates – encouraged by your kind letter – are now very well disposed to my plan for laying out the Oxford Parks & I have little doubt that it will be

The concluding illustration from James Bateman's Orchidaceae of Mexico and Guatemala. *'For the tail-piece Lady GREY of Groby has kindly contributed a most ingenious device, compounded of divers Orchidaceous flowers, which, with very gentle violence, have been induced to assume the attitudes in which they appear below.'*

carried in its integrity.' In fact they asked for one or two modifications – the deletion of an ornamental piece of water and of an arcade by the cricket ground which Bateman had seen as a venue for flower shows – before adopting the plan in 1864, 'gratefully acknowledging their obligation to Mr Bateman for the talent, zeal and assiduity which he has shown in the endeavour to carry out what the delegates understood was in the Mind of Convocation'. Robert Marnock, landscape designer and curator of Regent's Park, was appointed to supervise the work. Bateman's framework remains though there have been substantial changes to the planting over the years as well as other changes. In 1867 he entered a competition for the layout of Sefton Park, Liverpool, but was not successful.

In 1865 the Batemans' eldest son, John, had married the Hon. Jessy Caroline, daughter of the Hon. Richard Bootle-Wilbraham MP, 1st Baron Skelmersdale, and had gone to live in what remained of Knypersley Hall. When his parents took Cooke's house in London, John and Jessy probably moved into Biddulph Grange. It was not long before Bateman decided to hand over Biddulph as well as the Knypersley estate to John in return for an annual sum, and it must have been a disappointment for James and Maria when John announced that he wished to sell both estates and move elsewhere. James explained the reasons for John's decision to abandon Biddulph Grange in a letter to Rowland Egerton-Warburton in 1870. It was 'partly because he thinks it too large & partly (& much more) because he is constantly amazed by the perpetually advancing tide of population which renders game-preserving almost hopeless & quietude out of the question'. There was an additional problem of mortgages of £35,000 on the Biddulph property, for James had spent more on it than was perhaps wise. The entry in Cooke's diary for 24 September 1869 reads 'Mr Bateman wrote a sad letter', probably breaking the news of the decision to sell Biddulph Grange. In Bateman's letter to his brother-in-law he put a brave face on it, saying that, after all, it was 'a new – as distinguished from an old family – place' and adding: 'I only wish now that I had not laid out so much money upon it.' It failed to sell at auction in 1871, but was bought in 1872 by Robert Heath, the leading local industrialist, who had acquired 600 acres of the Knypersley estate three years earlier.

After paying off the debts John Bateman was still able to buy a large estate at Brightlingsea in Essex. He is best remembered as the author of a book which was once well thumbed by the mothers of eligible daughters. First published in 1876 as *The Acre-ocracy of England*, it reappeared in the following year as *The Great Landowners of Great Britain and Ireland*. In it were listed, in alphabetical order, 'all owners of Three thousand acres and upwards, worth £3,000 a year in England, Scotland, Ireland & Wales, their income from land, college, club and services'. This was based on a survey called *The Modern Domesday Book*, which had attracted a great deal of attention. Intended to show that land ownership was broadly based, it in fact showed that property was largely concentrated in the hands of a rich élite. John's own entry in *The Great Landowners* indicates that he owned 2997 acres in Co. Mayo (perhaps through his wife), 1413 in Essex and 1 acre (Knypersley Hall) in Staffordshire.

The Batemans' second son, Rowland, spent many years as a missionary in India before returning to Biddulph in 1906 as Vicar, where he remained until 1915. Their two younger children, Robert and Katharine, moved to Hyde Park Gate with their parents. Katharine – after whom the clematis 'Miss Bateman' was named by George Jackman – did not stay there long, for in 1868 she married Ulick Ralph Burke, a barrister, Spanish scholar and novelist. Robert Bateman, who described himself as a painter, architect and gardener, owed much to Edward Cooke who took him on painting tours to Spain and Venice and frequently entertained him in London. Six of Robert's works were exhibited at the Royal Academy. He was also an occasional sculptor, as was his mother. He lived for some time at Biddulph Old Hall – there was, and is, a house there as well as a ruin – with his wife Octavia Caroline, the daughter of the Revd John Howard, Dean of Lichfield, and widow of the Revd Charles Wilbraham, son of Randle Wilbraham of Rode Hall, Cheshire. They subsequently moved to Benthall Hall in Shropshire, now owned by the National Trust, where they remodelled the garden, before finally settling at Nunney Delamere in Somerset. Robert's favourite sport was bowls. He had been brought up with bowling greens at Knypersley and Biddulph and introduced them at Benthall Hall and Nunney Delamere.

There were workmen at 9 Hyde Park Gate South for some time before the Batemans moved in, but what changes they made to the house and the garden is not recorded. It is unlikely that two such dedicated gardeners could have

The printer of the 1871 sale catalogue seems to have attempted to match the variety of the garden in his choice of type-faces.

Continuing a statement of the more noticeable beauties of the Grounds, there will be found

"THE PINETUM,"

Which is a Curved Walk, and makes the circuit of the Gardens, planted with irregularly arranged Mounds covered with Heather, crowned with an immense and valuable variety of English and Foreign Conifers, and backed by Yews and Hollies. Here will be seen groups of Deodars and Araucarias, Junipers, Cypress, Savin, Hollies, Abies Nobilis, Pines, specimen Oaks and Thorns, Cedars, and in fact an assemblage of rare Trees brought together and arranged with the necessary regard to colour, tone, shape, and background, which only the most consummate taste and love for Arboriculture, could be capable of

Producing a result which has hitherto been unmatched.

THE RHODODENDRON GROUND,

Devoted to American Plants, formed in the most luxuriant groups.

"THE GLEN"

In the humid recesses of which are grown all kinds of Aquatic Plants and Marshy Reeds, with its Nooks and Interstices filled with a series of nearly all the British, and many of the Hardy Exotic Species of Ferns.

THE STUMPERY,

A picturesque assemblage of Old Roots, Rugged Stems, and Stumps of Trees, in all their gnarled, contorted, and varied forms—a well-appreciated home for Ivies, Creepers, and Trailing Plants.

THE PARTERRES,

The numerous Banks and Beds of Flowers, some laid out with the most studied blending or contrasting of colours, others with a happy negligence, yet with the richness and variety of a Natural Mosaic.

The Lawns, Orchards, Open Spaces, Terraces, The Geometrical Garden,

THE ARBORETUM,

THE ROSE GARDEN, THE DAHLIA WALK,

THE CHESHIRE BLACK AND WHITE TIMBER COTTAGE,

THE LIME AVENUE,

THE BOWLING GREEN, THE QUOIT GROUND,

THE FIVE'S COURT, AND THE MUSIC HOUSE,

Are the remaining more Prominent Items in these delightful Gardens,

In which it may be said are happily combined the highest scientific and instructive characteristics with all that is pleasing and delightful in Garden Culture.

BY A PRIVATE WALK OF ABOUT THREE-QUARTERS OF A MILE,

PASSING THROUGH

A highly picturesque Ravine, with a romantic Waterfall and pretty Stream, with Old Mill House and Cottage thereon,

Ascending Steps cut in the sides of the Cliff, across Rustic Bridges, and through Shady Clumps of Wood.

accepted a ready-made garden without making changes, even one designed by Edward Cooke. Maria again had her own garden, and James was able to report to her brother in 1870: 'Maria is in very good form working away even now in her garden – with all the zest of former days.' Evidence that they now had to be more careful where money was concerned is found in an exchange of letters with Sir Joseph Hooker. When Sir Joseph wrote in 1878 to Bateman, among others, for a contribution to a publications fund, Bateman pleaded that reduced circumstances prevented him from responding as he would have wished. Hooker had referred in his letter to his own 'mite' of £50, to show the way, but Bateman replied that the most he could possibly manage would be £10. Even for that a second application would be necessary: 'If just at the end of the begging campaign you find a few dribbles might be useful to squeeze the amount, you know where one such is to be had, only it must be *anonymous* please.' At about the same time Maria wrote to her brother Rowland, asking if he could find them a horse for their brougham with 'a strong & healthy constitution – but so deficient in breeding as to be worth only 50 or 60 £'.

Maria Bateman's constitution was the cause of a further upheaval for the Batemans, for Worthing was recommended to her as 'a prophylactic against Bronchitis', and they moved there in 1884. James began to plan his new garden before they left Hyde Park Gate South (they had dropped The Ferns from the address) and to look for plants, 'especially such as are likely to enjoy the peculiar climate of the place. This, judging from the condition of a few typical plants must be exceptionally favourable.' He particularly asked Sir Joseph Hooker for seeds of Australian plants, including eucalyptus, and he offered to report to Kew on the progress of any plants he was given. The response was generous, and by December he had several acacias in flower. In the following year he wrote to W. T. Thistleton-Dyer, who had then succeeded his father-in-law as Director of Kew: 'Of the 100 plants which Sir Joseph so kindly sent me about this time last year I think I could show you at least 95.'

The house the Batemans bought in Worthing, Home House (now Ridley House) in Farncombe Road, was a small villa with a garden of modest size, surrounded by the gardens of their neighbours. Although they were both in their seventies their enthusiasm for gardening was undiminished, and by 1890 they had once again created a garden which was acclaimed in the *Gardeners' Chronicle*. 'The more one looks at it the more surprising does it appear that a flat and desolate wilderness could be transformed into such a little paradise in the short space of six years.'

Once again picturesque scenery was created to provide suitable conditions for particular plants. Since the garden was exposed to strong winds from the south-west Bateman constructed a miniature mountain range to provide the necessary shelter. 'On the other sides of the mountain-pasture, called the lawn, rise in a semi-circle undulating mounds with winding walks between, rustic bridges vaulting over cavernous valleys, tunnels which suggest the galleries on

Lilium batemanniae, named in 1879 after Maria Bateman, 'a well-known liliophile and one of the first possessors of this kind'. The illustration is from The Garden.

the Simplon route, and picturesque gorges, while above all tower Ivy-covered rocks, whose jagged weather-worn peaks do not indeed reach the snow-line, but extend well above the region of the forests.' In the lee of this ingenious wind-break James and Maria Bateman were able to grow successfully some of the plants which had disappointed them at Biddulph, including his favourite Sikkim rhododendrons and moutan peonies, along with many other shrubs, herbaceous plants and rock plants. *Lilium batemanniae* featured among the lilies, a tall deep apricot Japanese hybrid which was named in 1879 after Mrs Bateman, 'a well-known liliophile and one of the first possessors of this kind'. No doubt 'Mrs James Bateman' (purple) and 'Miss Bateman' (white, with a faint green stripe, a chocolate throat and red anthers) were present among the clematis. The latter is still in cultivation. Although the article does not mention one, there must have been a conservatory for acacias to flower in December. It would be surprising if there were not also orchids.

'You know we have set up a mock range of mountains', wrote Bateman to Thistleton-Dyer, 'with the object of doing Homage to the Himalayan Rhododendrons & this makes us the more anxious to give them the companionship of other plants from the same region.' Prompted by Mrs Bateman, he was particularly asking for 'a morsel of that lovely little *Aster Stracheyi* (figured in the last No. of *The Garden*) which has journeyed from the Himalayas to Kew whenever it can be spared'. In another letter he asked for a palm: 'I crave your assistance in a delicate matter, which is none other than finding a husband for a *Chamaerops* Palm.'

Mrs Bateman continued to play a vital part. 'Where both Mr and Mrs

Clematis 'Miss Bateman', named after the Batemans' daughter Katharine by the nurseryman George Jackman, is still in cultivation.

Bateman have been in such thorough co-operation throughout, it would be difficult, and perhaps not altogether gracious, to attempt to discriminate the work of the one from that of the other. The co-operation is, however, patent and the result delightful.' Bateman was still trying to improve his garden when the author of a further article in the *Gardeners' Chronicle* visited Home House in 1894. 'We found the venerable artist had just descended from the highest altitude, where he had been rearranging a peak which had not quite pleased him.'

Maria Bateman died in Worthing on 4 May 1895. A little surprisingly James married again in the following year and lived with his second wife, Ann (efforts to identify her have so far proved fruitless), at Spring Bank, Victoria Road, Worthing, where he died on 27 November 1897 aged eighty-six. He was buried nearby at Broadwater. The year before his death he would have learned with sorrow that the house he had built half a century before had been largely destroyed by fire.

Robert Heath, Bateman's successor at Biddulph Grange, was one of the best known figures of his day in North Staffordshire and one of its most successful industrialists. He had earned a reputation for buying unsuccessful undertakings and making them profitable, and when he moved into the Grange he owned twenty-eight coal and ironstone mines, eight blast furnaces and many other enterprises. He was MP for Stoke in the 1870s and the High Sheriff of Staffordshire in 1885. He had been a friend of the Batemans for a number of years, and when John Bateman died in 1858, he was a member of the committee which was formed to perpetuate the memory of John and his wife Elizabeth. The almshouses they decided to build near Biddulph Grange 'for the comfort of poor widows and aged persons' are now badly in need of restoration.

As soon as he had acquired the Grange, Heath brought in the leading interior designers John Gregory Crace & Son to decorate the principal rooms. This was the firm chosen by Queen Victoria to redecorate a suite of rooms at Windsor Castle for the visit of Napoleon III in 1855, and they had previously undertaken work for George III, George IV (including the Royal Pavilion at Brighton) and William IV. Their watercolour designs for Biddulph Grange are an important record, and the one surviving room – Heath's drawing-room – makes the subsequent loss of so much of Bateman's house all the more regrettable.

While Robert Heath did not have the same deep interest in gardening as his predecessor, it is clear from late nineteenth-century photographs in the family albums that he maintained the garden to a high standard. Repairs to the Chinese temple were carried out in the 1870s, and, at about the same time, he replaced the old drive with a new approach from the then recently made Grange Road, while the road to Congleton was moved much further away from the house. The large yews and hollies along the drive today were probably transplanted from the old drive, whose course to the Congleton road across the present

Robert Heath, a leading industrialist and MP for Stoke in the 1870s, bought Biddulph Grange in 1872.

A scheme of decoration for the dining-room at Biddulph Grange by John Gregory Crace & Son, 1873, prepared for Robert Heath following his purchase of the house.

Grange Road is still marked by the tall pines which Bateman planted there.

When Robert Heath died in 1893 his eldest surviving son, also Robert Heath, inherited the Grange. He decided on extensive internal alterations before moving from Greenway Bank, Knypersley, where he was then living. When the work was almost completed a fire broke out during the night and destroyed a large part of the building. A new house was designed by the architect Thomas Bower of Nantwich, whose practice continues as Bower, Edleston and Mattin. The rather heavy renaissance baronial style does not blend altogether happily with the surviving Italianate wings of Bateman's house. The fine stained glass in the hall and by the stairs dates from this rebuilding. Of particular interest are the representations of industrial and scientific scenes – a coal-mine, a pottery, a rolling mill in an ironworks, a laboratory, an electric generator and an observatory (see p. 50).

Luke Pointon, a young under-gardener in 1861, was head gardener to both the Robert Heaths, as well as owning a nursery at Spring Grove, his home opposite Biddulph Church. His pocket diary for 1898 has survived, and the brief entries are a valuable record of the year's work in the garden. Much of it was routine – pruning, dressing walks with weedkiller, extensive repairs to the bottom of the pool in China – but there was also considerable new planting, while many existing trees and shrubs were moved from one part of the garden to another. Some of the transplanted trees were very large and the work took

three days – a day to get the tree out of the ground, a day to move it and a day to replant it. Surviving photographs provide impressive evidence of the size of trees Luke Pointon and the men he directed were able to move.

Photographs of Biddulph Grange published in *Country Life* in 1905 confirm the very high standard of maintenance the garden received under the Heaths, and this continued for another decade, but the First World War was a watershed in the history of British gardens. Many large and elaborate gardens which had been immaculately maintained until 1914 now proved to be beyond the means of their owners, and so it was with Biddulph Grange. The industrial enterprises of Robert Heath & Sons were no longer as successful as they had been, the farms and woodland owned by the family were sold, and Robert Heath went to live in Barlaston, south of the Potteries. In 1921 he offered Biddulph Grange to the North Staffordshire Cripples Aid Society for conversion to an orthopaedic hospital. The Society hesitated at first because of the cost involved in the conversion, but in 1923 Heath conveyed the house and the land to the Trustees of the Staffordshire Orthopaedic Hospital, and the new hospital was opened by the Prince of Wales on 14 June 1924. Unfortunately it was soon in financial difficulties and closed within a year. In April 1926 it was bought by the Lancashire Education Committee as a hospital for crippled children. It enjoyed a considerable reputation and must have been one of the pleasantest hospitals in the country. None could have had a finer garden.

ABOVE *Luke Pointon, Robert Heath's head gardener, supervising the moving of a large tree, an operation which usually took three days to accomplish.*

ABOVE LEFT *The fire at Biddulph Grange on 16 January 1896, photographed after the event with the flames restored by an artist and the fire brigade posing for the camera.*

151

EIGHT

Decline and Resurrection

When Biddulph Grange became a hospital the garden near the house suffered drastic changes. The upper terrace, the eastern terrace with its music room, the rose parterre, the verbena parterre, the cherry orchard and the dahlia walk were all lost as ward extensions were built at the east end of the house and the terraces to the south were simplified. But the rest of the garden continued to be maintained for the next sixty years by three able head gardeners – Bill Shufflebotham, Fred Hancock and Eric Bowers – and their staff, and much is owed to their dedication.

The great problem of the last twenty years has been vandalism. Access has always been difficult to control, and the secluded nature of several parts of the garden has enabled uninvited visitors to escape notice outside the working hours of the gardeners. With such an adventure playground on their doorstep, it is not surprising that local children and young people were tempted to trespass. Most of them came and went without causing any damage, but a few found amusement in breaking trees and in attempting to demolish the Chinese temple and other structures. After surviving so well for more than a century the garden quickly became a depressing place to visit and there were fears that it might disappear altogether.

In 1976 a steering group was formed with the object of establishing an association which would lease the garden from the Health Authority and restore it. In spite of the sympathetic interest of some of its officers, negotiations with the Authority were protracted, frustrating and fruitless, for the latter was not prepared to enter into the kind of long-term agreement which would have been necessary to secure the permanent survival of the garden. Meanwhile no adequate measures were taken to protect it from vandals.

The campaign to draw attention to the importance of Biddulph Grange continued. At the suggestion of the Garden History Society it was made a Conservation Area by Staffordshire County Council. The Royal Botanical and Horticultural Society of Manchester and the Northern Counties funded a botanical survey of the garden by the late Dr Mark Smith of the University of Bristol Botanic Garden. Articles appeared in *The Garden*, *The Observer* and *Country Life*. It was featured in three television programmes and was selected by the Post Office to appear on one of the four stamps issued in 1983 in celebration of British gardens. Its importance received official recognition when it was accorded Grade One status in the national Register of Gardens by the Historic Buildings and Monuments Commission.

When the Health Authority decided to phase out the hospital and to sell the house and the land it did not occur to members of the steering group that the National Trust might be interested, since the Trust usually expects to receive properties as gifts accompanied by substantial endowments for their future upkeep. Fortunately the Trust's officers and its Gardens Panel recognised the outstanding importance of the garden and urged that it should be acquired. With the promise of considerable support from the National Heritage Fund, the Trust took the brave decision to try to acquire the garden in spite of the fact that much more money would still have to be raised. Even then the uncertainty continued while the Regional Health Authority deliberated whether to accept the bid from the Staffordshire Moorlands District Council, who wished to acquire the whole of the Biddulph Grange estate and to pass on the garden to the Trust, or to take a higher bid from a speculator who wanted to turn the house into a retirement home. Perhaps the article which appeared in *The Times* at the crucial moment, expressing the hope that the Trust's bid would be successful, helped to ensure a favourable outcome.

Considerable progress has already been made with the restoration of the garden and it has been particularly exciting to follow the work on the formal gardens near the house. Although early photographs give a good impression of their general appearance before they were obliterated in the 1920s, more detailed information was essential, and the Trust commissioned an archaeologist to undertake an extensive excavation of the terraces. When the turf was removed and the soil beneath trowelled away, the bare bones of these lost gardens were spectacularly revealed and a great deal of information about their construction was obtained. The araucaria, verbena, rose and lower parterres as well as part of the dahlia walk were uncovered in this way. Much of the dahlia walk lay under a deep layer of spoil deposited when the terraces were levelled, and this could only be removed with the aid of a mechanical excavator.

This excavation gave further proof of the quality of the workmanship at Biddulph Grange. The paths were made to last. A layer of coal and clinker was placed in a trench and covered with small stones and grits, which in turn were covered with gravel and pebbles. The construction of the drains proved to be equally impressive. A highlight of the excavation was the discovery of the remains of the fountain and the site of a seat at the end of the dahlia walk. Although Edward Kemp had referred to Bateman's intention to install a fountain (designed by Cooke), there had been no evidence that it ever materialised.

As a result of changes Bateman made in the 1860s, when he replaced the

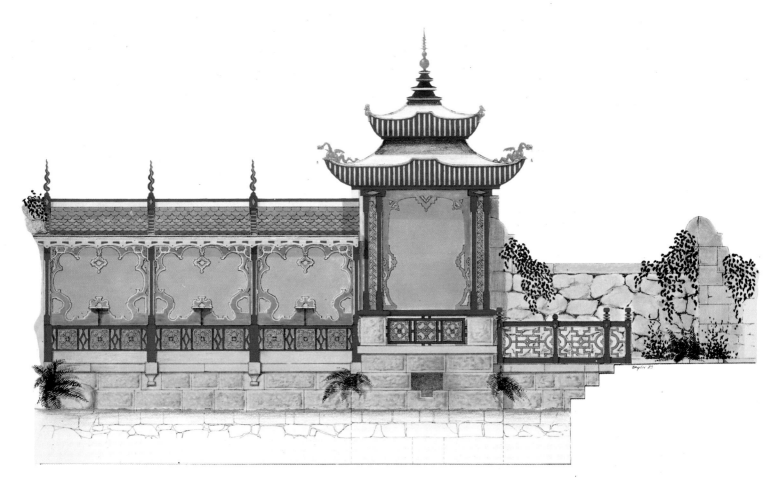

The front elevation of the
Chinese temple as drawn for
the restoration. The colours
chosen by Bateman and
Cooke were established by
scraping through the layers
of paint, some of the original
Minton Hollins roof tiles
were discovered at the bottom
of the ice-house, and the
remains of dragons and grebes
were found in the Chinese
water.

mosaic parterre, the araucaria parterre and parts of the dahlia walk and of Mrs
Bateman's garden with three grassed terraces descending to the lake, the house
became a more important element in the composition. Since most of the
original building is now lost, it was proposed that Bateman's earlier and more
formal scheme should be restored. It is very satisfying to see these long
forgotten gardens taking shape again.

The major architectural features of the landscaped areas of the garden – the
Cheshire cottage, the Chinese temple and bridge, the Wall of China and the
watch-tower – have already been restored. The original colours of the Chinese
temple were determined by scraping away the later layers of paint, while some
of the original Minton Hollins roof tiles – yellow, blue-green and black – were
found at the bottom of the pit in the ice-house nearby. So too was one of the
carved grebes, now restored to the roof.

The replanting of the garden under the Trust's head gardener Nigel Davis is
progressing well. Only plants known to have been planted by Bateman or
those which were then available and are likely to have been present in the
garden, even though they were not recorded, will be used. Tracking down
sufficient stock will be a major task. No doubt Bateman's prejudice against
hybrids will be borne in mind. The only planting not designed to recreate his
garden will be the screening of modern developments and other unsightly
features where these obtrude in the view.

It will not be possible, of course, to restore every detail of the garden exactly as it was. Although Biddulph is well documented, some features were not completely recorded, while the presence of mature trees, inhibiting growth in their vicinity, may make it impossible to replace some of the plants from Bateman's scheme during their lifetime. Some later planting, where it harmonises with the rest, will be retained, at least in the short and medium term – indeed, it is not always possible to be sure what was planted by Bateman and what by the Heaths. One or two of Bateman's trees which had grown out of scale with the garden have already been removed and replaced with young plants of the same species.

Replanting, unlike architectural restoration, can never be complete, for planting must be followed by the continuing process of maintenance. Shrubs and trees may require feeding, pruning, replanting and then, when they grow old, replacing. Only by continuous observation and sympathetic and sensitive upkeep can great gardens survive. Changes occur all the time, and for those who are able to pay repeated visits to Biddulph there will always be something new to see.

The site of the hothouses at Knypersley, once the main scene of Bateman's horticultural activity, is now a garden centre and little survives from the Bateman era. Perhaps the National Trust will eventually be able to introduce greenhouses at Biddulph so that visitors may see some of the orchids, tropical fruits, Sikkim rhododendrons, moutan peonies and other plants which brought fame to Bateman and his garden.

Biddulph Grange is one of the nineteenth century's really outstanding and innovative gardens. The originality and charm of its picturesque scenes; the telling use of surprise; the accomplished rock-work; the extraordinary topiary of the Egyptian court; the admirable landscaping of the pinetum; the unique Chinese garden; the variety of the plants and the skill shown in their cultivation – all these attributes set Biddulph Grange far apart from almost every other garden of the period. In their use of traditional hardy herbaceous plants and native plants from fields and hedgerows, James and Maria Bateman were forerunners of William Robinson and Gertrude Jekyll, whose campaign for a return to nature in the garden led to the sensitive informal planting which is characteristic of modern British gardening at its best; while the skilful and imaginative division of the Batemans' garden into a number of ingeniously linked areas, each with its own character and each offering a different setting for plants, helped prepare the ground for Hidcote, Sissinghurst and other great gardens of the twentieth century.

Not long ago it seemed that the Biddulph Grange garden would be irretrievably lost. Now, thanks to the intervention of the National Trust, it will again delight its many visitors, as it did a century and more ago, and will remain a lasting monument to the wit, the invention and the energy of its remarkable makers.

List of Sources

Manuscripts in the following collections

Arley Hall; Chatsworth Settlement Trust; Cheshire County Record Office; C. R. Cooke, OBE; London Borough of Hackney Archives; Herbarium Library, Kew; Linnean Society; Royal Society; Society of Antiquaries; Staffordshire County Record Office.

Periodicals and Newspapers

Botanical Cabinet; Botanical Magazine; Gardeners' Chronicle; Gardener's Magazine; Orchid Review; Proceedings of the Royal Horticultural Society; Staffordshire Advertiser; Staffordshire Gazette; Staffordshire Mercury

Other published sources

BATEMAN, James, *The Orchidaceae of Mexico and Guatemala*, 1837–43.

BATEMAN, James, *A Monograph of Odontoglossum*, 1864–74.

BATEMAN, James, *A Second Century of Orchidaceous Plants*, 1867.

BATEY, Mavis, *Oxford Gardens*, Oxford, 1982.

COATS, Alice, *The Quest for Plants*, 1963.

CORMACK, Patrick, *Oriental Architecture in the West*, 1979.

DESMOND, Ray, *Dictionary of British and Irish Botanists and Horticulturists*, 1977.

DESMOND, Ray, *A Celebration of Flowers*, 1987.

DON, W. G., *Memoirs of the Don Family*, 1897.

DOUGLAS, David, *Journal 1823–27*, 1959.

ELLIOTT, Brent, *Victorian Gardens*, 1986.

FERRIS, Ann, *Biddulph Grange*, 2nd edition, 1980.

FLETCHER, H. R., *The Story of the Royal Horticultural Society 1804–1968*, 1969.

FORTUNE, Robert, *Wanderings in China*, 1847.

FORTUNE, Robert, *Journey to Tea Countries of China*, 1852.

KEMP, Edward, *How to lay out a Garden*, 3rd edition, 1864.

KENNEDY, Joseph (editor), *Biddulph (by the 'Diggings')*, 1980.

LOUDON, John Claudius, *An Encyclopaedia of Gardening*, 1834.

LOUDON, John Claudius, *The Suburban Gardener and Villa Companion*, 1838.

MOSZYNSKI, August Fryderyk, *Rozprawa o ogrodownictwie angielskim* (1774), Warsaw, 1977.

MUNDAY, John, 'E. W. Cooke, Marine Painter', *Mariner's Mirror*, 1967.

MURRAY, Andrew, *The Book of the Royal Horticultural Society*, 1863.

MUSSON, A. E. and ROBINSON, Eric, *Science and Technology in the Industrial Revolution*, Manchester, 1969.

Sale Catalogue of Biddulph Grange and Knypersley Estates, 1871.

WIEBERSON, Dora, *The Picturesque Garden in France*, Princeton, 1978.

Unpublished source

LEAR, Michael and WOODS, Beverley, *Biddulph Grange Garden*, Historial Research and Survey Report, 1987.

Index

References in italic refer to illustration captions

Illustration Sources and Acknowledgments

A-Z Collection pp. 16, 44, 90, 91, 106, 110, 112 (below), 118, 121; Anthony Blacklay and Associates pp. 74, 75, 154 (Philip Taylor); British Library p. 34; British Museum p. 85; Linda Burgess p. 148; Christie's p. 150; C. R. Cooke OBE pp. 7, 37, 40, 135, 138; Robert Copeland and Mr F. W. H. Coles p. 63; *Country Life* p. 78; courtesy of the Hon. Michael Flower pp. 9, 99, 122; Martyn Gregory p. 141; Peter Hayden title-page, pp. 20, 43, 50, 61, 84 (right), 97, 102, 109, 112 (above), 132; A. F. Kersting pp. 130, 131; The Lindley Library pp. 21, 22, 23, 24, 27, 29, 30, 35, 39, 41, 42, 46, 49, 52, 53, 54, 56, 57, 59, 79, 81, 88, 105, 107, 111, 113, 115, 143, 147, 149; London Borough of Hackney p. 32; Mrs Joyce Machin p. 151 (right); National Maritime Museum p. 67; The National Trust pp. 12 (*Country Life*), 18, 77 (*Country Life*), 84 (left) (*Country Life*), 89, 127 (courtesy of Mr and Mrs James Fletcher), 151 (left) (courtesy of Mr and Mrs James Fletcher); Natural Science Photos p. 47; courtesy of Mrs Jean Stevens and the Redfern Gallery, London pp. 82–3; Victoria and Albert Museum p. 65; Mike Williams pp. 11, 26, 64, 87, 92–3, 95; William Salt Library, Stafford pp. 71, 73, 76, 101, 125, 145.